undividing

undividing
returning to oneness
for the first time

conor detwiler

Undividing

Returning to Oneness for the First Time

Copyright © 2020 by Conor Detwiler

All rights reserved. No part of this book may be scanned, uploaded, reproduced, distributed, or transmitted in any form or by any means whatsoever without written permission from the author, except in the case of brief quotations embodied in critical articles and reviews.

Published 2020

Library of Congress Control Number: 2020905470

ISBN 978-1-7347857-0-8 (paperback)
ISBN 978-1-7347857-1-5 (ebook)

Conor Detwiler
Scituate, MA
www.conordetwiler.com
inquiry@conordetwiler.com

For Nana and Papa, Grammy and Bumpa, Mom and Dad,
who brought us into warmth and beauty

*A thousand leaves glitter at the sun
where roots are cloaked, covered in mud.*

*In the stillness of a hardened seed,
a waking point—
silence breaks to living color.*

*In the quiet of your own awareness,
a flash of recognition—
the world takes to life.*

CONTENTS

INTRODUCTION — xi

CONTEXT — xvii

CONSCIOUSNESS — 1
THE HUMAN RANGE — 4
THE PLAY OF CONSCIOUSNESS — 7

AWAKENING — 13
THE ATEMPORAL JOY OF REALIZATION — 15
THE TEMPORAL PATH OF REALIZATION — 17
MEANING IN CONFLICT — 21
NO MAN'S LAND — 24
THE TEMPTATIONS OF FATALISM AND OPTIMISM — 26
FIXED AND SEARCHING PARADIGMS — 30
SUFFERING, PAIN, AND TRAUMA — 32

AWAKENING A NEW SOCIETY — 35
THE LIMITS OF BASER CONSCIOUSNESS — 35
RADICAL CONSERVATION — 41

CONNECTION — 45
LEARNING FROM NATURE: FLOW AS A CHOICE — 45
LOVE AND UNCONDITIONAL RELATIONSHIP — 51
AWAKENING THROUGH RELATIONSHIP — 56
AWAKENING THROUGH CREATIVITY, AND THE VOLATILITY OF AMBIVALENCE — 60

UNDIVIDING — 67
EAST AND WEST — 67
ORIGAMI AND UNFOLDING — 68
UNCHAINING CAUSALITY — 72
UNDIVIDING KNOWLEDGE — 75
BEYOND METHOD OR RELIGION — 82

THE INFINITE SPHERE — 85
HUMAN DEVELOPMENT AND THE INFINITE SPHERE — 86
CHAKRAS — 93
BOUNDARIES — 100
JUSTICE — 104

THE UNION OF FORM AND FORMLESSNESS — 111
ONENESS — 111
SEEING THROUGH INNER RESISTANCE — 115
BLISS IN POLARITY: FORM AND FORMLESSNESS — 115
THE EXPERIENCE OF PRESENCE — 123
PRACTICING AWARENESS — 125

ACKNOWLEDGEMENTS — 129

INTRODUCTION

There's nothing in a name. Except in the deepest sense, who I am has very little to do with this book's content. But in this age of the influencer even good things need a name and face behind them to push them into the world, and a brief description of the spiritual trajectory of my life may help you to understand the focus of this book. To give these pages tangible witness, to anchor them in the reality of human life, I will take you plainly into a sincere imagining of my past.

Childhood was alive with the constant exploration of a boundless, inward dimension. I thought that everyone perceived such a space within, and that the adult world must have been even more aware of it than I was. As basic to my understanding of growing up as going to school or learning about the world, deepening this inward realization felt like my primary responsibility as I prepared for adulthood. I imagined that any functional adult must be fully realized, but in many ways the opposite turned out to be true. Following this inward sense I found myself increasingly out of sync with the norms around me, and my adolescence—coming up

undividing

against the reality of an unconscious world and its pressures, systems that operated without awareness of this interior dimension—was particularly volatile.

I did not understand that spirituality could be so messy. Nor did those around me. As I looked for support and a way through confusion, my life was given a new context—that of modern psychiatry. The path of awakening I had stumbled through during my childhood was cut short and repressed, and I learned to relate to it as a disorder. I was heavily medicated through my teenage years and did what I could to adapt myself to the new circumstances of adult paradigms and systems.

Almost a decade later, after prioritizing survival and shutting down internally, I came to a point of such inner density and suffering that I realized I would soon take my life or make my own path to resolution. The adults around me, with best intentions, had tried to keep me afloat in the world but had blocked an inescapable process within. I stopped taking all my medications. When I told my psychiatrist, she advised against it, characterizing the decision as a symptom of my disorder. After I thanked her and hung up the phone we never spoke again.

The gates of hell were opened. I went through physical withdrawal, but the psychological burden of opening repression was much more intense. I had nightmares every night, and my days were filled with paranoia. I had trouble remembering basic things about my past and often unknowingly repeated the same sentence twice. I suffered frequent panic attacks that came in waves and would shut myself in the nearest bathroom to quietly explode. I must have looked crazy to those around me.

introduction

And yet I had a deep sense of purpose. I would move through all this repression and come to the peace I sensed on the other side. I would not shrink from a disturbing process: the resolution of spiritual awakening had become necessary for my survival. I gave myself to disorder and dysfunction and let things fall apart. I nurtured a quiet center within, a small but persistent bud of clarity, and gave up trying to be reasonable. Over the course of integration, I moved to another country and married a former monk. I made changes and upset people, and was left with only the friends who understood my intentions.

After nearly ten more years of resolute inward focus, I was in a new world. I had crossed through the darkness of collapse and distortion and come to a clearing, a bright and steady place. Now the joy I had always sensed beneath all things gave rise to the simple forms around me. An endless space had again opened within, a crystalline sense of meaning, an ineffable, living freedom.

I have lived through the disorientation of the awakening process twice: once in childhood and again in early adulthood. This book is focused on that process, and on bridging the gulf between the demands of the world and resolution in the spirit. It is a sort of spiritual blueprint that might have helped me through a difficult time, and I hope it will be useful to someone else.

But this book is meant for anyone who looks within. You will find that only its contours and the accident of its framing pertain to my particular experience; while it may be informed by a personal narrative, it is not about me. Whether you are engaging in meditation or active introspection for the first time or have spent years on a spiritual path, this book is about you. It is entirely defined by what value it has to you, the reader, and how it resonates in you.

If, not through logic, but through an inner quiet of discernment, you find its words genuine, or if they somehow buzz in you, then read on—even where a chapter is difficult or foreign. If you don't trust your gut to discern authenticity, or don't know what that means, perhaps this book will help you get in touch with that awareness.

Beyond awakening in the individual, this book also focuses on the necessity of a spiritual shift in our species. We find ourselves at a time in history when the demands of survival and awakening are one, not just for some of us, but for all of humanity. Collectively, we will awaken or perish. On a personal level, it is useful to understand both the roots and the magnitude of our collective dysfunction in order to navigate a path through that dysfunction and take part in this fundamental paradigm shift beginning to occur on the planet. Often, looking into darkness can help us make out light.

Where this book is abstract or intellectual, it is so in order to integrate the mind's questions and the complexity of our world into presence. If you want to connect to its real meaning, read it from the heart, from your depths, and in your whole body, allowing it to move in you. Don't get caught up in what doesn't make sense to you. All the details are only fruit for reflection meant to point to the experience of inward awareness, which is all that really matters.

That said, in a misinterpretation of contemporary spiritual teachings, many spiritual circles today perceive the mind as a natural adversary of awakening. Certainly, the intellect disconnected from its root and out of touch with an underlying experience of consciousness is a powerful source of delusion. Like the fictional image of a vampire, the disconnected intellect is somewhat cold, cut off from simple sincerity. But the intellect guided by awakened consciousness has created beautiful expressions of art, storytelling, and sacred architecture, and countless useful and inspired technologies across the world. We have become lost in our minds, putting the cart before the horse, but the mind in itself is no more an adversary than the proverbial cart. When it ceases to run our lives and is instead led by inward awareness, it is a wonderful tool.

For the scientifically inclined, it may be worth mentioning that this book refers to *the formless*, *space*, and *spacetime* interchangeably. Where such terms are used, they are meant to suggest nonexistence or nothingness. Many scientists today believe spacetime to be an existent something rather than the void perceived by the layman. But where this book refers to *the formless*, it is truly pointing to nothingness, and any slight property or somethingness that even spacetime might have (as perceived by many scientists) is here considered a subtle manifestation or veil of form.

In an age where most of us have limited free time and are adapted to constant streams of brief information, this book was written to be direct and concise. Pick it up and put it down in pieces. Fit it into your life, and read it when you have a moment to earnestly reflect on its content. Return to any part you don't fully understand or anything you find particularly meaningful. With repeated reading, as with any exercise, things will get easier and integrate more fully into your experience. Passages that may have seemed obscure will come to make more sense as you open more wholly to yourself.

After all, this book is for you. Its purpose is not to teach you anything you don't essentially know, but to help you realize what you already are. Feel it out, and use it as a tool for your own awakening and deepening sanity in a mad world.

CONTEXT

We find ourselves at a unique point in history. There is before and within us a sort of question, game, and gamble that pertains not only to our species but also, more essentially, to the universe itself. Though, for many, life carries on as usual, we see around us the signs of great challenges to come. The past centuries of the evolution of human thought and activity have yielded explosive development and material progress. Since the Scientific Revolution and the application of many of its methods and discoveries through industrialization, we have found ourselves capable of previously unimaginable levels of control over our environment, and in developed areas that have most directly benefited from this adventurous movement of expansion, general material standards are higher than ever before. Those so fortunate have more freedom from pain and privation than might have been imagined possible on such a scale just three hundred years ago. In a sense, we modern citizens are rulers of the earth.

But our reign is wearing thin. Our technologies, as any tools, have as much destructive as creative potential, and in the recesses of our minds the potential for global conflict on a modern scale takes on apocalyptic dimensions. Meanwhile, and just as significantly, the unintended consequences of many best intentions exhaust the planet on which we live, and the distribution of our industrial gains is dramatically uneven. It is clear to many that if war doesn't destroy us, climate change will, and the ever-increasing technological amplification of short-sighted and partial desires may prove as destructive as our capacity for outright violence. Amid such monumental existential threats, if we dare to appraise them soberly, we must wonder what meaning we have as a species, when such a great run of growth and expansionism buckles in on itself and our very cleverness seems to spite us. We may seem victims of our own success, and, in a sense, we are. If such a wondrous age of exploration now seems to have borne questionable fruits, what is our purpose? Have all our efforts been in vain if now their resultant gains threaten, or even seem to negate, our continuity as a species? What is left for us when our dreams become nightmares?

In essence, that is the question facing us now. Though many continue to hope that further expansionism and scientific progress will fend off the looming threats of our day as they have once and again in days past, it is clear that growth will not stem growth. At a time when we are most endangered by our own power—when our species has outgrown a sustainable place on earth and overpopulation and technological sophistication are our greatest existential threats—the expansion of that same power will not ultimately save us. So we are pressed to come to both a different understanding of ourselves as people and a different sense of purpose and meaning. We face a precipice, a limit to the continuity of our current paradigm. In this Anthropocene Epoch of human rule, we will fall or find it in ourselves to take flight.

CONSCIOUSNESS

Who are we, really? Who are you? It may seem like a simple question at first. I know who I am, you may think. Perhaps you do. But were we sitting face to face, could you tell me? If you come from an English-speaking society, you might start with your occupation. I'm a *blank*, you might say. Perhaps you are, now. But is that you? The same you who was once a crying baby, then a shouting toddler, a son or daughter, a sibling or cousin, then a friend, a student, an athlete or artist? Is each of these incarnations a new you? Or are you continuous, and these only conditions, temporary roles and forms that you inhabit? If there is some continuous you beyond these roles, what is it? Is it your body? But that can't be, because that's always different. You likely wouldn't be mistaken for a toddler if you're able to read this page, and yet, at one time, you took such form. So this real you can't be the changing body, not ultimately.

Is this you, then, your personality or character? But the personality also takes many incarnations over time. So we can say, I remember when you were an awkward adolescent or an angry teenager, or perhaps, I remember him or her before Alzheimer's or brain damage. Your personality inevitably varies, however subtly, over time, and your memory, even if sound, overwrites details, confuses, and imagines. Perhaps you feel that despite those changes there is some basic constancy, some persistence of a healthy sense of self. But doesn't that sense of self itself change over time, at least as it is strengthened or weakened by circumstances? Fortunate circumstances or fruitful effort can improve your self-esteem, shifting your self-perception. Unfortunate circumstances might degrade your self-esteem, shifting your self-perception. Many habits and preferences vary with the years. Beyond that, your identity is formed and adapted to each change in your environment, and a move to a very different society would set your behavior against different social expectations, different perceptions of gender, different standards of beauty and even constructs of time, making weaknesses of many perceived strengths and strengths of perceived weaknesses.

Each day, each moment, you are inevitably subtly different, down to an atomic level. Yet even as you read words that deny you as so many parts—that point to the fragility, or delusion, of your stable existence—you know that you are. You could read on about your nonexistence, but something in you knows itself, knows that it is. On some level, no matter what is said, you are, and there is nothing to finally refute it. You are deeper than anything that can be affirmed or denied, and that plain awareness of being outlives any temporary role or form you inhabit. It is not any thing in you that is constant, but that *you* itself, that being. Ultimately, the only constancy is being itself, what you know you are. It is upon that ultimately unnamable experience of self—of being, of knowing that you are—that all of the temporary circumstances of body and personality rest, and in which they find continuous meaning. It is upon that background of self-awareness, or consciousness, that all ephemeral form takes place.

That self is undivided, formless. It is you, essentially. It is just the awareness of being—of being you, of life, of being alive. There are no adequate words—here they are almost nonsensical—and yet on some level, we can all feel this to be true; we know that somehow we exist, that presently, we are.

It is because this essential being that we are is undivided and unchanging that we experience a paradox of time. We are here, now. And as this essential self, this being undivided by circumstance or time, we will also be there. The self is here, now, and the same self is there, later. There are no total gaps in our awareness, no total gaps in the continuity of time, no total gaps in our sense of being or self. The being that we are can be sensed in every moment because it's always there, unchanging. The ground of awareness that knows that it is, that exists beyond all temporal conditions, is every now. So today I know that tomorrow will come and, in the same undivided moment, the same undivided awareness, soon know tomorrow as today. So I can know now that my vacation will end in two weeks, and in the same now, two weeks later, my vacation has ended. Circumstances change, and so time takes form, but we are always here, and it is always this same underlying moment, this same awareness of being. So, essentially, we are this moment, beyond its temporal forms, and this moment extends through all time, since there is nothing to divide it. Therein is the eternity of being, of the spirit, and self-awareness unborn and undying.

This awareness of awareness is spirituality. As we look inward, feeling out our essential being beyond form and circumstance, realizing that we are, we become conscious of the consciousness that we are. On such an essential level, our very humanity is as relative as personality, age, or occupation. So our human search for meaning is not really human, but something more essential. We are the undivided nature of the entire universe coming to perceive itself as such through human form. We are limitless awareness becoming aware of itself, beyond all the shifting conditions of beginnings and endings. This simple realization of immeasurable depth is the visceral sense of substance we're all looking for. It is at the core of our inexhaustible search for meaning, and our evolutionary purpose.

The Human Range

This nearly incommunicable self-knowing of consciousness is timeless, since it pertains to a dimension beyond shifting situations, beyond change. As such it has been pointed to at all stages of human history by poets, painters, monks, hermits, and wanderers—any who have deeply felt the impulse toward self-realization and responded to it on a scale that defined their outward trajectories. So the artist will often throw away the world to express some sense of inward truth through varied form, and the sage is known to seek a simple context that doesn't compete with contemplative communion. From Soto Zen founder Dogen in thirteenth century Japan, to Bohemian-Austrian poet Rilke and Indian philosopher Sri Aurobindo at the turn of the twentieth, to Persian

Sufi poet Attar of Nishapur and German polymath Saint Hildegard of Bingen in the twelfth, to Einstein in the twentieth, to Sor Juana Inés de la Cruz in seventeenth century Mexico, to Saint Augustine in North Africa in the fourth and fifth centuries, to Chinese philosopher Chuang Tzu in the fourth century BCE, to Eckhart Tolle today. Really, there can be no linear order, no chronology of truth. That timeless knowing is a sea into which all the happenings of history dip, to varied depths. The human story is, from this perspective, the amorphous birth pangs of self-realization and the promise of new life. We have seen awakening in individual glimmers and collective contractions but have yet to see our whole world turn in upon its own light, and we still approach the day when all, as one field, might burst into decisive bloom.

Such is the full potential of our species, and its aim. And yet we see in ourselves a range of states and motives. We are not realized, not "perfect;" that much we know. Humanity has evolved from primates, and a cursory glance at evolutionary psychology suggests that we owe many of our raw impulses to that heritage. We are complicated, moved by all sorts of conflicting drives. In overt individual forms and subtle collective and systemic forms, we are driven by greed, jealousy, anger, revenge, lust, ambition, or general self-interest. These vices—framed by Abrahamic paradigms as base and evil instincts—look in an evolutionary light more like practical instincts that have served a purpose in the survival and strength of our species, the healthy pulse of natural selection. If that is so, and if, as it seems, the flourishing of industry through modern capitalism has depended upon a related pragmatism—the organized uninterruption of this human will to thrive, even through divisive competition and short-sighted egoism—then these drives cannot be so simply denounced, and that is the ambiguity to which much contemporary thought directs us.

And yet every sense of meaning, across cultures and history, points toward the realization of some ideal state beyond selfishness and petty conflict. Harmony, peace, abundance, ease, joy—the general image of heaven, in any society—is what we are all striving for, if only for ourselves. This orientation is inborn, because it is the vague expression of consciousness' self-seeking. The desire within us to feel good, resolved, and at ease can find its end only in the full self-realization of the awareness that we are, because only such a realization of essential oneness is personally or collectively sustainable.

The endless pursuit of pleasure or satisfaction through contriving favorable conditions is ultimately futile, since conditions, no matter how well managed, are subject to change, and since even amid the most favorable context we soon find ourselves bored and dissatisfied, chasing new gains. So we have only to glance at the endless growth of a consumer market to see the futility of its own philosophy. Nothing is ever enough, and sustainable satisfaction never comes. What circumstance, what condition, whether material or psychological—whether pleasing to the senses, or mind and emotions—is lasting?

Globally, as long as we continue toward selfish or partial gains, toward the creation of private paradises of guarded wealth, each year with raised stakes and greater technological power, we will certainly see broadening destructive effects. Our pursuit of personal aims, of satisfaction or pleasure through constant growth and consumption of the limited resources of a finite planet, will bring us all to suffer the consequences of environmental waste and eventual scarcity, or of deepened inequality and heightened competition.

These unbounded instincts to survive and prosper have been, for us, a stepping stone. But we are reaching the limit of their utility, and humanity will not survive the continual amplification of our baser drives. We have come this far by the movement of murky impulses, but now we must evolve out of our animal inheritance, realizing something deeper.

THE PLAY OF CONSCIOUSNESS

This self-realization toward which our species is oriented has more than human significance. As we look inward, sensing the consciousness that we are, we can turn the same awareness upon the rest of the world and sense that it, too, is conscious. To anyone who loves quiet and finds some intangible company in the simplicity of solitude, a walk in the woods or a natural park is a rich experience. There is an aliveness and balance in nature that transcends any biological observation. With quiet attention, we come to perceive an infinite and senseless depth in the natural world that takes us into it, and more easily into ourselves. In the space of our own silence nature comes alive, flowering for and within us. Thousands of variegated shades of feeling come to our attention, swirling in eddies around cold rocks and pressing through verdant leaves as a crisp and dampened breeze.

Words can only touch the surface of such natural harmonies, and something like poetry may be the best symbol for their delicate intricacies. Any human art seems crude beside the impossible subtlety of the natural world and its countless expressions, patterns, and tones. In any moment of such appreciation and careful attention, we sense that the real substance of nature, or its essence, is not different from our own, and that we are only one of its countless manifestations.

And yet we are unique. A rock is rugged and uncomplicated, but inert. A plant is alive, but does not know itself to be. Sunflowers have enough awareness of their surroundings to turn toward the sun and many plants shift from day to night, but can't question why they do so nor reflect on their activity. Insects flee from danger and strive for survival, in their own ways attracting mates or entrapping prey, sometimes even with creative cunning. But they don't do so with intention or choice, because they don't have the reflective awareness to consciously weigh their options. Animals, from reptiles to mammals, fight to protect their young, perhaps mate for life, push across continents for food or procreation, and many clearly experience a vast range of emotions and whims: grief and fear, bonding and play. They have memories and preferences, and distinct personalities. Many domesticated animals may learn to understand the patterns of a human family and integrate themselves right into our lives, at times reminding us of our own small children. Even more intelligent animals invent tools to make their lives easier and engage in problem-solving. Capuchin monkeys use rocks to crack coconuts, and aquarium octopi have been known to cleverly escape their cages. This implies a level of reflection, of awareness of conditions and a dip into abstraction, considering not only what is, but what could be. Dolphins and chimpanzees are even more aware, and they are able to communicate with physical and vocal languages and recognize their own reflections in a mirror. Not only are they abstractly conscious of their surroundings, but of themselves: they can perceive that they exist. Still, no animal can reflect on its own existence. No animal can consider what it is to be, or not to be, and no animal shows signs of existential angst or a search for meaning.

It is for this reason that we consider animals amoral. They are not able to reflect on the causes of suffering, individual or collective, and come to sustainable oneness. A tiger cannot change its stripes. While nature manifests profound balance, it is also marked by stunning brutality and desperate competition. It entails the inevitable frenzy of the battle for survival, of tearing another animal apart, or perhaps of living, like a harmless rabbit, in a constant state of alert lest such a fate devour you. It allows the unrestrained fight for dominance and the unapologetic preference for the victor. Such behavior in humans is quickly recognized as brutish and grotesque. Where the animal has no choice but to follow the course of its instincts and so acts without what might be called moral consideration, the human does conceivably have a choice. It is within the range of human expression to be as brutal as any animal, and even more so, as our greater sophistication can be moved by cruelty or callousness. But it is also within the human range to find freedom from all these brutal impulses and to use that same sophistication to serve all of our needs, potentially, in an enlightened future, liberating ourselves entirely from the consideration of survival or competition and resting in an abundance of united community.

This range of possibility makes humanity a moral species, with its dark side gripped by brutal and competitive impulses and its full realization an expression of connection and oneness extending beyond all personal considerations, embracing all animals, plants, and mountains—and all of existence—in its loving gaze. Humanity may be the only species on this planet with the capacity to realize fully what it is beyond its form. If all the signs of evolution point toward greater consciousness, with more evolved species showing more awareness of their environments, and thus more self-awareness (as their surroundings share their own basic nature), then it isn't vainly anthropocentric to say that, in our known world, humans are the fullest expression of this universal impulse to awaken. If consciousness expresses itself through all forms and species, it is through humans that it can become fully self-aware.

That is the difficulty of being human. We exist between two poles that have often been called *human* and *divine*, and may also be called unconscious and conscious. The struggle for self-awareness in any one of us is the same evolutionary struggle that has pushed all of life toward greater consciousness. We experience this struggle consciously. So our art depicts it in all its varied forms. Our tragedies express its seeming impossibility, and our comedies make light of it. We are able to see that our most unconscious and destructive impulses may destroy us before we come to collective realization, and today that is a source of much distress. There is no certainty that we will come to realize a utopia of self-awareness, and only when this inward evolutionary struggle is collectively transcended, or at least recognized as such, is any utopia possible.

Our reflective capacity for deduction and problem-solving has given us modern science and enabled material abundance in the most developed areas of our world, freeing many from the outright struggle for survival and relief from pain. But that reflective capacity has not yet turned in on itself, reaching through egoism to the living experience of unconditional self. Until such collective realization, even our great capacity for problem-solving will inevitably find itself duped by self-defeating and unconscious projections and fear or apathy toward some imagined *other*. So we find ourselves divided from one another and from nature, and it is quite possible, in this confused state of grasping for relief and fulfillment, that our race will end before such realization. That question depends on each of us.

AWAKENING

What is it to pause, and look within? So there is really no fixed identity of self, no constant entity that we are. Yet, we are. How can we come to clearly sense that essential being? First, simply stop, and notice. Notice any sensations—subtle or heavy feelings within you and a physical experience of the world around you. Notice your breathing, and its inevitable continuity. You can hold it for a time but, sooner or later, it will resume. Notice any tensions in your body. Notice the space around you, and notice silence. Notice the sounds that rest on silence, and the forms that rest in space. Notice silence in sounds, and space in form. (Is every sound pure density and force, or is there a softness behind it? Is every form a fixed entity, or is there some receptivity to it?) Notice space in yourself, behind thoughts and sensations. And notice the thoughts that probably carry on over the canvas of you—the awareness that you are. You don't need to abandon thinking or try to stop it—just zoom out a bit. Disinvest from it. Thoughts are ephemeral. Like the changing body, they can't be you. Like the many shifting emotions or physical sensations you may have observed, they can't be you. Shift your awareness from your thoughts to an intangible sense of being, of you.

You are the space behind form, whether internal or external. You are the space behind tensions and thoughts. Therein is a constant measure of peace beyond circumstance. What do you notice, looking within? It may not be so profound, at first. Perhaps, as you pause, you just feel a bit relaxed. Perhaps you notice some warmth or contentment. Or perhaps you notice some anxiety or discomfort. Whatever it is you feel, or don't, move into it with your attention. Let it be, and be it deeply.

Maybe these words sound like nonsense, and in a sense, they are. Look to their practical meaning. Take them as a guide to inner action. There is no perfect way to guide a person with words to flex their arms (if that instruction alone doesn't make sense; if they have no bodily comprehension of the action). There is no perfect way to guide a person to unflex their arms if those words alone aren't enough. Likewise there is no perfect way to guide a person to unflex their mind, body, and emotions, and open inwardly. But that is not because such motion is essentially difficult, it is because it's an organic and visceral action and can't really be described in logical steps or pieces. Just as you might engage any muscle in the body (even an atrophied one)—plainly and directly, the way we engage all of our muscles, the way we will physical movement—you might look within to engage a simple experience of awareness. Take this cue, and feel it out for yourself. There is no perfect way, but the continued intention alone, however imperfect, is bound to move in you.

Like a river through rock, any organic motion is bound

to open what's hard and reach the self more deeply, even if imperceptibly. In that sense, the imperfect action is perfect, and the mess and ambiguity of an unclear inward focus are exactly what they should be, because they are organic, because they come from you, and because each of us is different. As every form in nature thrives by its own idiosyncrasy, so spiritual awakening in each person will have its own particularities, even as the essential impulse toward the realization of consciousness in each of us is the same. Just as there can't ultimately be a uniform method for creating art or falling in love, there cannot ultimately be a method for coming to self-awareness. We can't really systematize organic processes, can't patent any path into the depths of ourselves. Simply recognize this raw inner impulse, this orientation toward meaning and realization, and make it your priority. Choose to move deeply inward, however that happens through you.

THE ATEMPORAL JOY OF REALIZATION

If we are collectively called toward spiritual awakening, what does that mean for us, personally? What does this awakening feel like? If it is, from some universal perspective, our human aim, why do we care; why "should" we "want" it? This inward movement ultimately yields an inner sense of expansiveness and freedom, and a playful, constant, and refreshing movement of vibrancy. As deeper and deeper inner doors open, as consciousness opens to itself, there is widening excitement and wonder, as though your sight had set for the first time on open ocean or the brightness of a piercing sky. Then there is space within, and a sense of play within that space, like splashing about in love itself. Warmth and intimacy kindle the clean glow of simple newness.

Such accessible and absolute liberty is probably absurd to consider without direct experience and must sound fantastical yet, at the same time, familiar. Universal depictions of varied heavens give form to that murky sense of what lies within us, and by that form we may imagine more clearly what pure consciousness feels like. But formal imaginings of heaven are superfluous, and their real value is in the sense of meaning they awaken within you. What is the root of that sense of meaning?

In such a reflective state, and in the light of heightened awareness, all things are alive. It is not only the natural world and the harmony of a forest that you come to sense as consciousness, as life. An immanent presence resonates in all things. An incomprehensible but vivid certainty marks a table, or a tile. Some closeness shines, some intimate familiarity, constant and acute. Inevitably, aliveness gleams everywhere. To the mind it makes little sense, and yet it is clearly felt. Beyond the separateness within you, everything is connectedness. Any ultimate emptiness that you perceive in the world has only ever been your projection. You confuse twists of apathy and deadness within you for apathy and deadness without.

If you are very still, you may feel it. Just a glimpse of such connectedness. Just a glimmer of intangible aliveness within. You might sense some energy or aliveness in your hands or arms, legs or feet, torso or head. You may feel some aliveness looking at art, listening to music, or being in nature.

Or you may not feel much of anything. You may feel a

bit tired or relaxed, or vaguely agitated. You may not have a clear experience of awakening or anything significant as you begin to get in touch with yourself. But there is no need to make deep inward experience a goal or destination. Just look within, seeing what arises, or doesn't. The sincerity of such intention alone is significant, and seeds an inward ground for the first sprout of clear activity.

The untying of tangled shoelaces requires a constant quiet of bright attention before the first string yields. The contented patience of a good fisherman makes way for a surfacing strike of flashing scales. Sooner or later, the intentional stillness of meditation incubates spontaneous inner movement as so many concepts and pointers come to life in your direct experience.

Make it a constant experiment, and play with that inward gaze. As you come to sense that intangible sense of self, of being, deepen your focus on it, come into it fully, and let the world and its infinite forms fade away. So, for moments, you come to know the world from the inside out, from its own heart. So you know the heart of the universe as your own and find yourself at one: undivided.

The Temporal Path of Realization

So, in moments of connectedness, you sense oneness. Then, most likely, you come back to the forms of the world and their demands. You probably have to focus on a job and invest yourself in its details. You may have to take care of children or others. You have relationships to navigate. You live with some level of conflict, overt or subtle: maybe stressful obligations, interpersonal tensions, frustrations, or situations you'd rather avoid. You have strong desires and disappointments. Connectedness fades, and the demands of living take you back into them. You are again invested in form.

Bringing one's whole life out of such investment is a process of deepening awareness. That process is not always smooth. It may even be filled with conflict. Opening to what's within means opening to it all. Everyone has long-held emotions and identifications. We all have some internal weight, or "baggage," we're carrying around. Letting it go can be very uncomfortable and messy. It's certainly neater, and may even look nicer on the surface, to keep your baggage packed and those underlying emotions tucked away, beyond conscious awareness or expression. But any tucked baggage will always come between you and the connectedness of the spirit and will unconsciously color your world. What you don't open to within will face you in disguise through varied projections. What you don't choose to see within you'll inadvertently imagine without. So life's subtle or overt dysfunction continues, and you continue to live amid so many problems.

Opening to it, though, can at first look like an even greater problem. Choosing to acknowledge your mess rather than push it aside can look and feel chaotic. Expressing how you really feel, being sincere, and giving breath to everything shut in can bring significant disorder. It may not be easy to tell your partner that you're frustrated with him when you don't even fully understand why yourself. It may not be comfortable to admit to a friend that you feel guilty about something you did when you don't know how she'll respond. Synthesis is not a neat process.

Most of us live through our minds, ordering our lives based on what we think they should be or what we want them to be. That allows us to function and keeps things "on track," as far as we can tell. It also keeps us from acting from the heart and separates us from authenticity. It keeps us living in controlled pockets of inward division. At times we may question why we continue as we do and what it's all about. Or we may feel called to change course, to find new purpose, perhaps through a new job or a move to another place. We can dismiss such rumblings as the inevitable dissatisfactions of being human—the human condition, as it were. Or we can pay attention to them, challenge the limitations of that apparent condition, and move toward authenticity and the ultimate satisfaction that we sense is, or should be, our nature.

Disengaging from the dominance of thought and underlying emotion and finding orientation in the self often entails many leaps of faith. The path you make with your mind has conceivable steps. It makes logical sense. But letting the inner sense of what you are and what you truly desire direct your life is, to the mind, a dead end. There are no steps in following one's heart. There is only a guiding glimmer, imperfectly understood. As you zoom out, or divest, from thought and emotion, and experience more deeply what you are, you will come to feel some direction, some aliveness, meaning, perhaps possibility. But this new orientation is irrational or, more accurately, transrational. Choosing to act from the undivided oneness of consciousness means acting from beyond the mind's calculations, from beyond the social guidelines of a world invested in its own sense of order, and forgoing a definable course.

So the process of bringing all the forms of life—relationships, work, and so on—into that deepening awareness, and so bringing undivided consciousness fully into daily reality, can often feel daunting, crazy, and irresponsible. The mind rebels; one's sense of order, of how things "should" be, often protests. Meanwhile, there may also be a sense of adventure and purpose, even something of a thrill.

Purpose that comes from the deepest self is what we often refer to as a dream, and most of us feel that the pursuit of a dream is in itself more meaningful than its end. In the classic capitalist myth, we do not root for those who have calculated their way toward material wealth or inherited it through due procedure. We root for the impossible, for the irrational and insurmountable. It is the authentic dream and courageous fidelity to inner guidance that makes the ultimate triumph of our hero more than material. Even the tragic hero who follows her heart but does not reach her material aims inspires.

Whether or not we recognize it, we sense that the meaning is not in the end, but in the "journey." We sense that the inward movement is far more significant than its outward fruits. At least we do as we hear or watch someone else's story. But coming into oneness ourselves, disinvesting from the dictates of apparently reasonable expectations, and letting our lives play themselves out beyond plans or a sense of control tends to feel like a different story. No clear beginning or end marks our path and no promise of resolution awaits, whether glorious or tragic. The mind stops at the unknown as we continue into the vague and slowly unfolding direction of the self.

Then we venture in small ways to "unpack baggage," to

give voice to silenced or ignored emotions and inner experience. We take a single step into the maze of a seemingly impossible conflict, be it in a romantic relationship or a political argument. You speak the first small words that you know to be true, but whose consequence you can't measure or contain. You find the courage to stand out or disagree, and find faith in the transcendent power of resolution. In other words, the inner knowing of oneness moves in us so as to draw all things into itself, patiently untying even the prickliest of knots within and between us. Here the mind would ask you to know better, and not to cross through such confusion. Yet the heart, the being, that intangible sense of meaning, draws us to press up against limits, testing them and believing in their ultimate dissolution.

So you fumble earnestly to express something difficult to a partner or friend, continuing to communicate through discomfort and hoping for an uncalculated resolution. So we come together in protest, assembling in the hopeful image of an unrealized ideal born of the depths of conscience and consciousness, and believe, despite the odds and status quo, that its time has come. So underlying being draws all things to itself, and we evolve messily, even calamitously, toward full self-awareness, beyond illusions of division born of unconscious identification with the forms of the world.

MEANING IN CONFLICT

Disengaging from the imposed direction and order of thoughts and moving into feeling, or a true sense of self, is disorienting. As we act more directly from a state of basic awareness, we set ourselves adrift. There the mind has no mooring, no bearing. When we stop counting and controlling so many pieces (which are ultimately only projections and approximations anyway), our sense of purpose stops amounting to anything. In undivided awareness there are no pieces, no amounts. We cease to know definitively "who we are" or "where we're going" as we come to experience ourselves beyond constructed identities. There is instead an aliveness of presence, an acute experience of being. For a time, though, as we surface unconscious pieces within, that presence expresses itself through a tangled filter of fragmented thoughts and emotions, and there may be significant confusion of direction, and inner conflict.

The opening of inner compartments, of inevitable discrepancies and dissonances, of confusion and irresolution, can be overwhelming. Whether we relax mental control by choice, or such control is overthrown by life circumstances, grief, or trauma, there can be some chaos within. This is a sort of inner anarchy, a stateless expanse between two senses of direction: that of our thoughts and unconscious emotions, and that of the true self, of undivided awareness underlying. So we may drift between some great sense of purpose or clear state of presence, and a torment of doubt and insecurity. We may feel connected to nature, to the world around us, and to others, and later be battered by an onslaught of negative thoughts and emotions. The reorientation of one's entire life into presence is, after all, a profound shift, involving the whole psyche and all of its conflicts.

Amid such conflict, in which some may live for years, the soonest resolution comes through heightened presence. Breathe intently, bringing yourself back into any connectedness you can feel. Root yourself in the inner awareness that shines a subtle, womblike vibrancy around any turmoil, making any disturbance a kind of parenthetical, submerging fragmented relativities into the quiet of observing consciousness. Focus intently on the observing self that always is, no matter what experience is playing over it.

As the movement toward self-awareness is our evolutionary impulse, there's no sense in attempting to move back into the familiar hold of thought dominance and ordered fragmentation, no sense trying to get a grip. The only way through it is through it. The mind struggles to control, to grasp, to understand this process in pieces. But thought cannot comprehend indivision, cannot comprehend non-separateness, infinity, eternity.

So you might shudder to find yourself surrounded by dark, open ocean, or the empty endlessness of outer space. Thought breaks everything into parts, but vast glimpses of oneness are always "mind-blowing," because they cannot be understood through fragmentation. They cannot be understood through thought, but they can be known through simple, undivided awareness. Your mind cannot understand oneness for the same reason your hand cannot grab itself: you cannot ultimately grasp what you are; you can only be it. So you come to know clearly what you are as you know that you are, and there is no final need for mental understanding. Moving continuously into that awareness, even while your mind may torment you, demanding a plan or explanation, is the only way through this dark wood.

No Man's Land

Many have had an experience of oneness and feel their purpose oriented toward it. We may have sensed a full and irrational stillness in meditation or spontaneously in another context—perhaps when wholly immersed in a sport or repetitive physical activity; perhaps when creating art or music, or deeply engaged in valued work; perhaps in the presence of beauty in nature or a spiritual environment; or maybe even as impossible conflict gave way to a sudden breather, an inadvertent moment of surrender. Still, we are aware of irresolution, both within and in our outer circumstances. In the light of deeper awareness, much of the world in its state of unconscious disorder becomes intolerable. The spiritual path is not always what most imagine it to be: one of acceptance, demure grace, and good behavior. On the contrary—there is often more spirit in the passionate vision of the revolutionary than in the good-mannered complacency of so many who hold blindly to the status quo. To see more clearly by the light of awakening consciousness ubiquitous injustice, apathy, cruelty, and suffering is challenging.

Greater self-awareness means greater awareness of the disorder both within and around you, and that can be hard to navigate. As you disinvest from thought-orientation and move to reconcile repressed emotions and complexes, identity and psyche into the awareness of the underlying self, things turn upside-down. As you make the underlying self the center of your reality, displacing structures of thought and belief, you are fundamentally changed and see the world around you through the looking-glass. This human world and its systems still revolve around thought and entrenched paradigms, and in the light of deepening awareness they start to look insane. So you find yourself, like Alice in Wonderland, among strange and sometimes alien social landscapes. As the inner resolution of the psyche into presence is a process, so is the outward resolution of one's place in the world. It is common to find oneself in a no man's land, fitting in nowhere. Aware of the potential for resolution but thoroughly unresolved. Moving inwards toward peace and harmony while lashing out in confusion along the way. Increasingly conscious of humanity's potential and frustrated by its limitations. With new hope for meaningful outer circumstances, perhaps more meaningful work and relationships, but unfulfilled.

Here Alice can be something of a guide in her state of dispassionate observation. Bringing your whole world into a deepening awakening is moving always from the controlled order of the mind into the vibrancy of intuited oneness. If, upside-down, you come against the insanity of the world, keep returning to a state of presence, of sensed oneness. Focus your attention always into the aliveness of that underlying resolution even as you burst, react, and come undone. You may have to allow yourself some disaster on your path inward, to give yourself the space to open your dysfunction into the light of consciousness. So witness the strange landscapes of this world, and of your own psyche, with plain awareness. Bring your attention back to connectedness even amid fragmentation. Through that conscious ground accept mess, accept irresolution, within and without; so take disintegration into yourself, dissolving it into the observing space that you essentially are.

In this transitional state, faith—an awareness of the

undividing

whole, yet to be fully realized—can be a patient guide. There is no sense in grasping at paradigms you know to be false or trying to force yourself back into the ordered surfaces of thought dominance. Instead, move further into the glint of the unknown with boldness and resilience. If you have seen glimpses of oneness and sense the resolution toward which you are oriented, return to a sense of that fullness as you face the inevitable challenges of integration. A constant aliveness of patience will work itself into the darkened corners of your world and, as constantly and coarsely as winter gives way to spring, resolution will come.

The Temptations of Fatalism and Optimism

As movement into the self can be so disorienting, the impulse to grab hold of something solid—of an apparently sturdy belief or paradigm—can at times be very strong. The kind of certainty that leaves no room for ambiguity or doubt is alluring, because it feels solid and stable. But, inwardly, to hold onto anything solid is really to hold oneself in a knot, to clench the psyche and deny the inward opening into presence. That very denial, that inward knot, can be strangely comfortable, because it serves as a kind of emotional shield. Such is the enchantment of determined despair, of cynicism and futility. If you grip the psyche tightly, you can create some pockets of near numbness, seemingly safe, icy spaces within that block out potential volatility of feeling and the discomfort of uncertainty.

Often, the psyche knots itself around painful experiences so that the fluidity of consciousness can't reach them

awakening

and you don't have to experience them fully. Emotions knotted and repressed within are shielded from your conscious experience and, in that sense, kept at bay. At the same time, they are knotted into your psyche and so embedded into your unconscious reality. They are gripped tightly as persistent tensions in your body and may be experienced as physical pain or even bring about illness. Those knots defy their own release into the simple connectedness of consciousness.

For example, you may have "shut down" during a difficult experience, whether of fear, anxiety, guilt, or shame, in an effort to shield yourself from it. Perhaps while being insulted or attacked, perhaps under pressure or after making a mistake you perceived to be consequential, perhaps while being bullied or ridiculed, you may have tightened up internally to block out difficult or overwhelming feeling. In the moment, blocking out such strong emotion may have allowed you to function within the dictates of the situation. So perhaps you were able to keep reading from the script in front of you during a nerve-wracking presentation rather than run out of the room, or you were able to keep your surface cool while someone insulted you rather than angrily explode or break down crying. Especially in the most sophisticated societies, there are many social codes that ask us not to express internal experience sincerely, and so compel inward division.

After you start to clench inwardly, knotting yourself within, attention and awareness will return to that inward tightness so as to move through it. The consciousness that you are, by its very nature, moves to resolve inner conflict and unflex constriction. So it will press against inner twists, bringing your mind back to originating experience. But this resolution asks you to experience the emotion you initially blocked out. If you reject this natural flow toward resolution in an effort to ignore or deny it, to continue to block out discomfort within, or even only through the simple belief that there is no way to move through it, that only "time heals all wounds" or that it's "better to let sleeping dogs lie," you might flex the psyche harder, constricting yourself more tightly in order to more thoroughly block out emotion.

Rather than open into the vulnerability of experience, you may close yourself to it with firm thoughts and beliefs. So you may "conclude" that "he is a terrible person" or "I never do anything right," or even something broadly bigoted like "all men are terrible" or "women are untrustworthy." Such conclusion is not really conclusive, but an imposed cap on your experience, the conceptual expression of an inner wall. This wall may bring you into greater stability—now you are somewhat partitioned from unpleasant emotion—but it is a deadened stability that divides you from yourself and keeps you in a state of biased disintegration. Such constriction blocks you from the clear perspective of the simple awareness that you are. It is the "great log in your eye" referenced by Jesus in his famous teaching on judgment: "why do you observe the splinter in your brother's eye and never notice the great log in your own? Take the log out of your own eye first, and then you will see clearly enough to take the splinter out of your brother's eye."

As you divest from form and shift your attention to the experience of your essential nature, divest also from these inner knots. The resolution of awakening presses you to move through such inward blockages, unflexing the psyche. Let these knots loosen, let your conscious awareness press up against them, let the false security of their tightened numbness dissolve, and come into contact with the underlying pain or difficult emotions.

As you allow yourself to consciously experience these tensions, they soften. Consciousness, like a flame, brushes against these blockages, and they come to slowly unravel and disintegrate in its light. So you slowly release an inadvertent, tightened inward grasp and open to your essential nature.

Depending on how much tension you hold within, this may be an intense or recurring process. Each knot will be unique in its structure and quality, but, as in the whole movement toward awakening, the basic experience is the same: when any knot starts to unravel and there are strong experiences of emotion or memories, return to presence, return to that simple vibrancy of observation, and let the particular contents of that moment resolve themselves into it.

Rather than cynicism, such inward knots might also be guarded by determined optimism or rigid positivity. If there is a hardness of perspective, even of "good vibes," there is likely an inward knot. Where there is no space for uncertainty and observation—for the simplicity of presence, of awareness—there is probably some inadvertent inward defense.

In your perspective, in your worldview, look for solid certainties, any hard sense that "the world is like this." Even determined optimism often forms to block out underlying fears or the uncomfortable ambiguity of uncertainty. Beyond their content, look for beliefs that express themselves as fixed. They are likely the conceptual expressions of inward knots, inward clenching, coloring your world with an almost imperceptible sense of limitation.

In the full awakening of consciousness, there is no beginning or end. The awareness underlying is undivided in space and time, formless. Where the mind perceives a definite end, whether of despair or salvation, there is almost certainly inward tightening, and the psyche likely knots itself, holding fast to illusion to insulate itself from hardship. As you seek out these knots, approach them with a living patience, unwinding and freeing yourself into the openness of your essential nature.

Fixed and Searching Paradigms

The semblance of solidity you grasp for, or create inwardly, may form to protect you from observing pain, but it may just as well form simply to keep you from the disorienting experience of the self.

If, like most, you have some fixed sense of the world, some relatively solid sense of direction or values, this is also an inadvertent obscuration of underlying awareness, albeit a more pleasant and stable one. In your paradigm, what is fixed, what is solid, what is certain, is not ultimately real. All conditions are temporary, all forms ephemeral. Even the forms that present themselves now to your awareness have no clear, solid basis: we know of no finally indivisible, minute particle, no fixed base of matter. So in all the universe there is really nothing to grab hold of. A meditation on that simple truth will cause some existential panic if you are invested in a false sense of solidity, as most everybody is. Such panic is a very natural prelude to release.

Where there is solidity in you, you are inadvertently blocking the true self, repressing the inalienable freedom and sense of meaning that you are. You are flexing yourself into a defined shape, causing a muscle cramp of the psyche, so to speak. Look into the certainties of your worldview, of your sense of direction, of your desires and plans, of hopes and dreams. Look for how things should be, when they should happen, and all that you try to control. Look for hardness of perspective.

Do not give up your sense of direction or your dreams, but yield to the substance, the feeling of them, beyond their conceptual content or apparent solidity. Behind the fixed forms of your desires and hopes there is essential authenticity. The levity of hope is ultimately real, but any fixed form it takes is a distortion, an entanglement of the buoyancy of your true nature. Do not give up faith, but its objects. This is a subtle distinction that is difficult to put into words, but feel for what is rigid, and see for yourself if it is truly real, or if it can be let go.

Where there is anything solid or determined, and especially anything that rejects or fears the reality of impermanence, see if you can unflex it with inward attention. Just as a massage heightens your experience of tension before relaxing it, such inward release may first cause some distress as your stable ground gives way. But the unknown is the reality of your situation and your self, whether you accept it or not.

As you open into it more deeply, letting go of a solid sense of your life and your self, you'll find that the unknown was more familiar, more known to you all along, and the security and identity you grasped at were only a carried burden. The simple, formless ground of being—the observer—is what you are and always have been. Releasing everything extra is an unfathomable relief.

Suffering, Pain, and Trauma

Some of us find ourselves in states of severe pain or trial, and look toward awakening as a desperate hope and a chance for release. If you are in such a state of suffering, know that there is release, there is resolution. There is nothing that can be written to sufficiently comfort the afflicted. There are no adequate words to free those living in a context of injustice or constant pain. A state of crushing depression or pounding pain can last for much longer than we would like to believe, and some of us live for years or decades with such a burden. Some live amid the blinding confusion of trauma and know what it is to watch their bodies and worlds seem to go on without them as past memories or doubts invade their experience and there is nowhere to find safety or rest. Others live with strict limitations imposed by chronic illness and may also be watching the forms of the world seem to carry on without them. We all have periods of illness, grief, and distress, where seemingly stable ground gives way and we feel abandoned by circumstance.

The inward path can be a desperate and determined fight. It is not always delicate or polite. Realizing more deeply your nature as consciousness is such a significant endeavor in any of us that, like a survival situation, like anything all-consuming, it transcends the dictates of context and reason. Especially if you are suffering and see no way out, awakening may happen in you as a fierce and absolute explosion toward freedom.

Often in a blinding state of pain you can't see what you're fighting for, and still your will moves you to continue. Look into that will, connect more deeply with it. Look into yourself and feel out your root. Practice meditation, however it happens for you. Look and connect inward, and know that all suffering can pass.

Suffering is a state of mental affliction, and that is a state of consciousness. All states of consciousness can be relieved through presence, even though that process can be very hard. So you may feel intense sadness and despair, anxiety or panic, or crippling anger. Such intensity of emotion can choke the psyche. Still, these are just very dense inward knots. Look for the aliveness in you—to the will that keeps you going—and focus clearly on it. That will is your center. It is the consciousness that can move to relieve all dissonant mental states as they resolve themselves into it, as you direct your awareness to them and trust in their release.

In heavy states of suffering this can be a very slow process, and resolution may be imperceptible. Keep moving inward and trust that there is subtle resolution happening even where it feels pointless. Every movement toward small, even seemingly trivial inner resolution counts. You are not imagining it, and the release you hope for is possible as you continue to lift one inner stone after another. You are deeper than any suffering you experience, even though that may seem impossible.

Pain, on the other hand, is not a state of consciousness, but a physical condition. Some pain or illness is the body's reflection of a fragmented state of consciousness and may be completely alleviated through presence. Some pain or illness is much more physical and originates in the body itself. Such pain or illness might not be relieved by inward awareness and might depend on medical treatment or symptom management.

Even so, the impulse to awaken transcends the human body and its conditions. The meaning of human life is not ultimately in its outward trajectory, but its inward realization. Through the human species the consciousness that you are seeks deepening self-realization, and even the body and its conditions are secondary to that fundamental universal impulse. So if you are able to read this page, you can look inward to realize that meaning, to open to the reality of your experience, to get more essentially in touch with yourself. The freedom, openness, and clarity of conscious awakening are more fundamental than the body, and they can be realized even underlying a hard physical state or condition. If you are suffering and life seems closed to you, look constantly within, and come to know in small pockets of hope that with continued inner movement, deeper freedom and aliveness are possible.

AWAKENING A NEW SOCIETY

The Limits of Baser Consciousness

Most of us still live, both individually and collectively, in a state of partiality and fragmentation. If we are truly one undivided consciousness, why do we live amid such a confusion of seemingly irreconcilable perspectives and collectively vacillate between tolerance and conflict, rarely experiencing synthesis or integration?

It seems that we are collectively coming to the limit of our animal consciousness, as it were. The impulse to survive and prosper is natural and is observed in all living things. The determined push of self-preservation—the will to live—is a vibrant expression of consciousness and a movement in its evolution toward self-realization. So people and animals generally experience a fighting rush and heightened state of awareness when threatened. There is some integrity in a living form that lends itself to the evolution of consciousness—the living body is a vehicle for consciousness' self-realization—but the perpetuation of that form is not an end in itself. Survival and prosperity are not ends in themselves. They are the foundations of evolution, of a deeper process within us. Still, collectively, we have not realized that.

Like very intelligent animals, we use our minds to solve problems and bring about prosperous conditions, and by our greater sophistication, born of greater awareness, do so more skillfully than any other species. So we have a limitless capacity for innovation and development. We can reason abstractly, imagine, and invent. To a greater degree than any animal, we know our circumstances to be relative. We are aware that they will change and that we can change them. We can, by and large, mold our environment to our own image.

But by that same abstract capacity and greater awareness we can generate endless subtleties of emotion, ideology, and belief. We can develop fixations and obsessions. We can repress ourselves and create complex and complicated systems. Unlike animals, we can cling to emotions and invest ourselves in thoughts and memories, fantasies and delusions. As a manifestation of more realized consciousness, humans have greater fluidity of choice and expression. We have a fuller freedom of will, by which we can spin ourselves into innumerable forms and frameworks.

So our deeper capacity for variety of creation has allowed us to produce a vast range of paradigms. There is, on the one hand, beauty in such diversity. There is wonder in the range of forms—of language and style, cuisine and culture, mythology and religion—that we have made. Inherent to the value of our species is the value of our creations. Yet we find ourselves, still, in a state of identification with all these forms. We have become entangled in our conscious and unconscious creations: in our memories, ideas, ideologies, identities, and complexes.

Many of us are very invested in a context of past experiences, in where we went to school and who we know, in grievances and long-standing conflicts with others, in professional identities or political ideologies, in national or religious identities, in positive and negative self-perceptions. Through humanity, our consciousness is free enough to generate great diversity but has not yet realized a deeper freedom, that of its essential self-realization beyond the multiplicity of its creations. We are conscious enough to imagine endlessly, and yet not conscious enough to realize that we are not, ultimately, those creations, but the creative consciousness itself.

As the harmonic buzz of the natural world gives way to brutal interruptions of ruthless self-preservation as animals fight for survival, the communal buzz of a city may just as well erupt into violence as humans fight for survival or the survival of their varied creations, whether physical or ideological. We may go to war, killing others to perpetuate the smooth functioning of our "way of life." We may be willing to do almost anything, to oppress and deny the rights of others, to keep afloat our own sense of "normalcy" and sensible reality. We often fight with the same passion for the survival of entrenched paradigms as we do for personal survival.

As we have developed cultures across all regions of the earth, and as we have such fluidity and freedom of will, our cultural expressions and belief systems are numerous and distinct. We have sophisticated religions, politics, philosophies, scientific theories, national identities. As our technologies become more sophisticated, boundaries of time and space between us shrink. With the printing press, relatively uniform ideas were spread across continents, sparking col-

undividing

lective movements of social upheaval and revolution. With the internet, we can just as easily communicate internationally as we can with our next-door neighbors or might just as easily order a book written two thousand years ago as one written this year. Ideas clash on a new scale, and our endless expressions of culture, art, and ideology confront one another.

Some "self-radicalize" with foreign propaganda, and through others international causes crystallize toward mutual ends. Weapons become more deadly and complex each year while defenses broaden. Walls are built and understandings are reached. Subtle rivalries and alliances are formed, and as ideologies multiply and fragment and weapons advance, we find ourselves amid increasingly delicate cold wars. We are, each day, more subtly fragmented and differentiated, even as we grow more aware of the potentially grave consequences of such fragmentation.

Pluralism, then, becomes a tenuous anchor for us all. The agreement to disagree and the coexistence of many disparate perspectives require that we step back, to some degree, from our worldviews, and recognize a common good beyond our separate intentions. We are generally able to see that radicalization, or absolute identification with any paradigm, may be deadly. With such technological capacity and a growing population, we are too close to one another, and too powerful, to act hubristically and indefinitely from our own limited frames of reference. We know that we have to share our space and our resources, and recognize commonality among us.

Meanwhile, as our capacity for communication has increased, so has ease of trade, and now even the most perishable commodities are regularly transported across the earth. Otherwise senseless movements of goods are justified by economic incentives, and an apple from across the world may be cheaper and more accessible to many than an apple grown a mile away. So even with the best intentions we tear up the natural world, sending metals and chemicals this way and that, strip mining and deforesting, and powering most of it with fuels that disrupt our earth. It is easy to sense something manic and maddening in this increasing speed and complexity, and, as we check the pulse of our planet and recognize that we are exhausting its patience, this sense is confirmed.

Even as the growing awareness of our circumstances moves us slowly toward a more sustainable use of resources (renewable electricity and responsible harvesting, fair trade and the protection of the natural world), any growth will ultimately prove unsustainable if it doesn't have at its heart a shift in our collective state of consciousness. The partiality of our aims and our entrenched paradigms will have to be transcended. Our human dysfunction is deeper than our methods, deeper than the ways we do things. The root of our dysfunction is in our collective state of consciousness, and its animal inheritance.

We are able to reflect and innovate, to find new ways of doing things that meet the demands of changing conditions, but, in the same way that animals lack the self-awareness to significantly reflect on and modify their conditions, we still lack the self-awareness to recognize that we are not any of the conditions that surround us—not those imposed by our environments, nor those we ourselves create. We are not our cultures, not our beliefs or religions, not our ideologies or identities, but something more essential and truly inalienable. We are the consciousness that, through human bodies, generates all this form. Until we reach through lukewarm and shaky truces of pluralism to its own beating heart, we will feel ourselves increasingly confined by compromise as we struggle to coexist amid ever greater differentiation and technological sophistication. We must delve into the heart of pluralism and so beyond it—into the heart of oneness, the heart of ourselves—and therein find not concession, but liberation. We must do more than compromise and prosper: we must awaken to ourselves, beyond form.

This awakening is like the shedding, or release, of a skin. As movement of global development continues, it comes to reach a natural limit. Our baser instincts, framed by much of modern psychology as the natural dissonance of human experience, are increasingly amplified until their dysfunction becomes evident: they are no longer serving us. The demands of survival on this planet today are different from those that have led us to this point. Many of us can see that our current state of affairs is unsustainable, and there is an impossible sense of confusion when we "do the math." Amid such great existential threats and such a halfhearted reaction, how will humanity survive? That limit, that very unknown that we face, and probably will come to face more directly as differentiation and sophistication increase, asks us to adapt in some essential way we don't understand. So it is, to our minds, truly a precipice. It defines the end of a worldview, but does little to hint at any possibility beyond it. That is because this adaptation asks us to go beyond the mind and take a leap. It asks us to evolve out of the partial and separate perspectives we currently understand as human and discover ourselves more deeply.

Radical Conservation

Awakening to the self beyond the forms of the world, to consciousness beyond its manifestations, is a natural impulse, and as such it is not essentially in conflict with what we have created as a species. Though spirituality and "the world" are often framed as mutually exclusive, they are not fundamentally so. The spirit is not contrary to the world, but beyond it—or so intimately inherent to it as to transcend its instabilities. Consciousness is the foundation of the universe, and spirituality is the direct and visceral experience of that basic reality.

While it is true that the full realization of ourselves as consciousness comes as we disinvest from thought, emotion, and form, there is no need to actively destroy what already exists. The existing structures of our world, whether social, political, economic, cultural, or otherwise, have arisen out of unsustainably biased aims and fragmented motivations, and some revolution is called for. That revolution, though, is a radical push to self-awareness, to the direct experience of our formless nature. This is not a destructive drive, but an intense impulse to reformation and a deepening sense of connectedness out of which new collective possibilities materialize.

Certainly humanity has, through a confused state of consciousness, created all manner of disturbing forms. We have manifested many nightmares, and something subtly nightmarish is built into the fabric of most of our social norms and institutions. In his most famous story Franz Kafka transforms the intangible alienation of our mechanistic systems into clear monstrosity as his breadwinning protagonist wakes up to find he has become a giant insect. Unable to continue providing for his family, his utility is exhausted, and he is treated as a burden and embarrassment. Those around him fail to recognize any unconditional value within him, any essential nature beyond his function. This is the inevitable result of conditional relationship, of the unawareness of essential reality beyond form. Any relationship based in thought, in ideas and expectations we have of each other, and not in an awareness of underlying unity, is on some level conditional. Ideas and expectations pertain to circumstances, and circumstances change. This great investment in thought and function makes up much of the social fabric of the highly industrialized world and accounts for its aura of alienation.

Despite their efficacy in elevating material standards of living, our industrialized systems and values, rooted in complex conceptual structures, are invested in circumstances and blind to the unconditionality of consciousness. While a world lost in thought has great power to develop and enhance, it is little self-aware. So its codes and norms may provide unparalleled security and comfort, but by their increasingly sophisticated conditionality, alienate in ever subtler ways. A film of distrust and insecurity coats all conditional relationship. A group linked by utility can be productive, but it cannot be communal—a community must come together inwardly and organically and know itself as one.

Be that as it may, the disturbing constructs of our world, and the many forms they take, have been created through confused filters of identification, through the obscured vantage points of unrealized consciousness. So the fastest way out is not to fixate on existing forms, continuing to shape ourselves into limited perspectives that obsess over ignorance, but to disinvest from them. We don't need to destroy anything, really. We just need to withdraw from, to release. If today all of humanity were to let go of its entrenched entanglement—ideologies, beliefs, conceptual identities, grievances—and let itself be moved by a transcendent push toward self-awareness and resolution, the nightmares of our world would disappear in little time.

There is in us, as in the universe itself, a natural tendency to create, to express forms. Where we connect to underlying consciousness, we create from beyond the mind and its limited paradigms. We express as one focal point of undivided awareness, and our actions have significance beyond our mental understanding. As thousands of ants create vast organic structures, each by the freedom of its own instincts, the modest work of each ant expressing itself clearly in the whole creation, so we, from a state of inner connectedness, might bring new and unimaginable conscious structures into our world. When we engage a state of simple awareness, we are moved to action whose significance we can't always clearly understand until, with time, it comes into discernible form. From our depths, even acting into an abyss, we start to bring a more meaningful new world into existence without fully understanding what it might look like.

As individuals, we can lead this movement of disentanglement by actively letting go, disinvesting from thought and circumstance. In presence we find release and the clarity to free ourselves from situations of discord and suffering. Some difficulty or conflict is inevitable as we make our way toward realization. But we can always choose to release more deeply, letting the forms of the world be and addressing their dysfunction at its root: the confused investment of consciousness in complexity. So the fragmented structures of the world are not the fundamental problem, but a symptom that collapses—as waves over water—into the simple persistence of awakening.

CONNECTION

LEARNING FROM NATURE: FLOW AS A CHOICE

As creation has, through us, expanded into such tremendous multiplicity—generating endless branches of knowledge and subtleties of identity, technological innovations and material abundance—we have become more entangled in it. As that multiplicity of creation continues to expand and our societies become more differentiated, we will only become more entangled. So we reach periods of collapse as this ever-increasing complexity of conflicting paradigms and personal aims buckles in on itself, as increasingly dissonant perspectives clash with increasing technological force. How can we cast off such complexity and come to a simpler and more essential awareness?

Here nature can be a guide. What can you sense beyond the surface of the natural world? What is it that attracts you to a flower or a bird, a beach, a park, or a walk in the woods? There is both an impossible complexity and an impossible simplicity in nature. Its surface is jagged and incalculable, messy and decaying, rough and porous. Were we to try to

undividing

form a clear image of any natural setting in our minds, with all its infinite, minute happenings—insect life, decaying twigs, sprouting plants, falling leaves—we would be overwhelmed. There is a lot happening, at any given time, anywhere in the natural world. Yet often we go into nature to unwind. Despite the frothing bustle of marine life—crabs flitting over salted sand and darting sidelong into tubular trenches as gulls angle for scraps overhead—we go to the beach to relax. Why aren't we moved to lay out our beach towels near shop windows on crowded downtown sidewalks at rush hour instead? Why is it that the stimulus of the natural world soothes, but the stimulus of traffic enervates?

Somehow we sense some beauty and harmony in nature. Despite its surface complexity, we sense something uncomplicated in it. Somehow, beyond its constantly changing face, it expresses a subtle timelessness, maintaining equilibrium through ceaseless self-renewal. It is always moving and adapting. Especially since the Industrial Revolution and the success of rapidly expanding technologies, we have turned a mechanical mind on everything around us, looking at the universe itself as a great system and, in that sense, a giant machine. We endeavor to understand the world through cause and effect, as many pieces that act on others and add up to bigger pieces. That has proved practically useful for arriving at a certain level of understanding of natural patterns (everything from thermodynamics to developmental psychology, geoscience to biochemistry) and for developing technologies. But if we look closely at nature, we see that it evades our grasp. It is always infinitely deeper than our logical understanding.

Any organic shape has an endless subtlety of line and

form. If we pick up a leaf and try to code an exact replica, we are bound to get it wrong as we look at it on an increasingly minute scale. In the image of our own mechanistic thought we have referred to the integrity of a natural setting as an ecosystem, but it is more than a system or a sum of parts. A close and connected observation of nature reveals something more like a Celtic knot: a form without end or beginning. Not a system, but a synthesis.

The natural world is a living synthesis and expression of oneness. Logically, this is impossible to prove, since the rational mind itself understands in pieces. But it is easily known through feeling. From a state of simple awareness disinvested from thought, it is easy to sense the intelligence underlying the natural world, and the balance brought about by this intelligence can be a guide to you. In deepening your awareness of the consciousness underlying the natural world, you deepen your awareness of your own inner world, as the consciousness within you and that expressed through the rest of the universe are not separate. You are not, ultimately, separate from nature: how could you be?

Nature is an easy portal to inward experience since it is a direct expression of the intelligent harmony and indivision of consciousness. The greater self-awareness in humans, and the fluidity of creation and relative freedom of will it implies, have paradoxically brought us to more confusion. We have a capacity to pursue selfish ends with such subtlety and technological amplification that even the brutality of a lion is refreshingly guileless beside our designs. Although the lion's self-seeking and our own human selfishness are ultimately expressions of the same state of unrealized consciousness, the sweeping shades of violence of which we are capable, even inadvertently, are more pernicious.

The balance of the natural world is an expression of undivided consciousness. If any species competes with the life of the whole, it will again find a sustainable place. So the overpopulation of any single species inevitably leads to starvation or predation, some movement toward balance. As consciousness approaches its self-realization through all forms, pushing always toward such evolution, it is as much invested in the totality as in any part—ultimately, the parts and the whole are the same. There is no whole without parts, as there are no parts without the whole. The push of life through forms, the evolution of consciousness, presses each species to thrive to its greatest capacity, regardless of the consequences that its success might entail. The lion hunts and procreates, willed toward its own abundance, and does not concern itself with overpopulation: it simply starves when the time comes. All forms, thriving together, create mutual limits, inadvertently maintaining equilibrium.

We humans are different, and yet the same. Our greater awareness allows us to pursue our own gains at the expense of the whole, which is why only we are capable of what we call artifice. Plastics strike us as particularly artificial because they are refined beyond a sustainable place in nature. They serve our ends, but do not fit into the whole. Yet what we call artifice is, ultimately, not entirely unnatural. The impulse to thrive is not unique to humans, and if lions or apes could create plastic tools, they probably would. No other species can, however, create the complexity of overpopulated imbalance that we can, because no other species has sufficient consciousness or intelligence to so dramatically fulfill its partial will.

This presents us with a challenge, which necessitates our awakening. On a broad enough timeline, we humans are not exceptional, in that we cannot, ultimately, usurp universal balance. If we continue to thrive as short-sightedly as we do now, we will certainly bring about our own end, or at least radically reduce our population, and the planet will, with time, reestablish equilibrium. So we are as much subject to natural balance as lions, or sunflowers, or any life-form. Because we are a more realized expression of consciousness, we have greater power to extend this timeline and to cause more collective destruction. But the consequences of our partial success will be the same, in order if not in magnitude, as those of any other species: we are currently laying the groundwork for our own self-destruction, and the rebalancing of the whole.

There is in our species, however, one essential difference from any other. At the highest end of our human range, we have the capacity to become conscious of ourselves as the whole and choose its balance as our own. Unlike other species, which live this balance, but are not conscious of it—which are often brutally pressed into sustainable form by the force of the whole, through starvation or predation—we can become aware of ourselves as the harmony underlying all things. We can choose to live from awareness of the whole rather than be blindly subject to it. We can awaken from unconsciousness rather than suffer its consequences.

In nature, we can look to such harmony to sense the underlying awareness that we are. The natural world is not confused by such a drastic state of imbalance as are our human societies because it remains a general representation of universal intelligence. The partiality of any other species

undividing

is less powerful than our own, so, except in acute moments of attack and survival, fades into the background of general unity. Beyond humans, there is no species with enough sophistication to usurp the general manifestation of oneness for any extended time. Stepping out from our complex and yet-unchecked self-seeking and into the balance of the natural world, it is easier to sense the oneness behind all things.

Yet despite its balance, the natural world is not fundamentally self-aware and cannot reflect on its existence. It is, but does not know that it is. It doesn't have the virtue nor burden of human self-awareness, nor the more conscious functions of abstraction and reflection on past and future. Animals don't fixate or repress and, unless domesticated into the imbalance of our current state, don't display neurosis. An animal lives what it lives, while it happens. When it experiences pain it cries out, when it is happy it is entirely so, and it lives out grief or trauma plainly. An animal doesn't need to be counseled to accept abrupt change or challenging conditions. It doesn't need to choose to face its experience because it doesn't have the option of avoiding its experience. It doesn't have the reflective capacities in which we can become so entrapped, twisting ourselves into regrets about the past or anxiety about the future. A three-legged dog is just that: a three-legged dog. It does not feel that it is missing a leg or have to practice acceptance of its situation; it simply lives naturally in its new state. It does not know that it lives as such a clear expression of consciousness, but it does.

This default state of presence expressed by animals or plants can help us perceive what it is to disengage from all the complexity of our human investment in thought and fixation. Looking into that clear state of unhindered experience, we get a direct sense of the simplicity of pure awareness. By contrast, we can see everything extra in ourselves, all the complication that we grip tightly. As we see nature's simplicity, and notice, by contrast, our own inward burden, we may more easily choose to let it go. We can continually take this action to come to a clearer state of awareness, observing simplicity and making the conscious choice to enter more wholly into it. So through us—as us—consciousness makes a great leap: first evolving out of the animal state of unreflective awareness into human abstraction and a greater reflection on conditions, and finally turning that reflective capacity directly upon its own self-awakening.

LOVE AND UNCONDITIONAL RELATIONSHIP

As we connect to the undivided self underlying, we come to sense it in all forms. Everything is an expression of consciousness, of being. We can sense nature's presence and the qualitative presence of other people. As humans, we are deeper, or more self-aware, manifestations of consciousness, and such consciousness has more potent variety of expression. While our shared humanity implies similarity between us, we are also marked by differences. More fundamentally, we are all expressions of one conscious ground, but in us that ground expresses itself in countless formations. So people display a vast range of personalities and temperaments, drives and desires. So in some people there are heavy inner burdens, in some little self-awareness, in some personal warmth, in some charisma. Some are quick to anger, some are melancholic, some are passionate, some are quiet. Regardless of the manifestation, of the particular expression of each person, ultimately we are all expressions of the same fundamental essence woven into a variety of forms.

We all have preferences and aversions, likes and dislikes. Some of those may be conditioned by experience, complexes that we can dissolve through awareness, but many are just the characteristics of our form. Just as we have different bodies, we have different personalities and preferences. So we are attracted to different music, different cultures, different people. We have different sexual orientations and different interests. As we deepen awareness of the underlying self, those particularities don't disappear, but express themselves more naturally, without our identification or entanglement. So we don't ultimately experience ourselves as body, personality, or preferences, but instead experience a formless, vibrant sense of self expressing itself freely and unreservedly through the unique form that we relatively are.

Most deeply, every human is consciousness itself, but on a less essential level is also that particular person. Coming to know ourselves beyond form, beyond individuality, paradoxically allows us greater freedom to express our natural uniqueness. But we don't need to have any thoughts of who we are, any focus on identity. We already are who we are, are unique—it is impossible for us not to be. Without inner entanglement we are free to laugh as we do, speak as we do, love as we do, walk as we do, and simply to live through our unique form however it happens naturally. Therein is individuality without separateness.

As we come to know ourselves beyond form and live plainly through whatever we are more relatively, we act from beyond mental conditioning, and our expression is authentic.

Then, that same awareness of the undivided self that allows us to experience and express our relative uniqueness freely also allows us to experience the relative uniqueness of others from such an unconditional space. So we experience the vast range of human possibilities, of different personalities and characters, from an inalienable sense of oneness with the heart of the person, the consciousness beyond the form.

Most of the time, others will not be so self-aware, as the current evolutionary state of consciousness of humanity is still not generally awakened to itself. So you'll notice that while you may come to sense oneness with others, and some underlying consciousness as their essence, they may not be aware of such an inner dimension. You may see consciousness twisted into knots and identified with all sorts of manufactured paradigms, often with heavy burdens of repressed emotions, "vibes" that color your experience of that person. It is often easy to see burdens that others may themselves not be consciously aware of and clear emotions they express without realizing that they do. So some people are very pleasant to be around, and some, by the weight of such inner twists and burdens, are very unpleasant.

Just as you observe entanglement of thought and emotion within yourself, you may observe others express from such unconscious identification. So you may notice others express from an unquestioned alignment with collective paradigms: with cultural or political ideologies, or perhaps with social norms and expectations. You may notice them express from an identification with past experiences, projecting repressed or unresolved emotions onto you and others. Or you may simply notice others relate to the world through a mind-filter out of touch with the unconditionality in and around them.

How many of our interactions are the projections of inner distortion—of emotional baggage or identification with the mind?

If, beyond any surface manifestation, we are an undivided ground of consciousness, then what between us is truly personal? We are awareness meeting awareness. The rest is either relative or the senseless noise of entangled confusion. None of the conflict we experience is ultimately personal, because none of it emerges from the deep simplicity that we are. Wherever we disengage from inner confusion and relate from a state of presence, an underlying sense of connectedness persists, even if others don't realize it.

This is the base of unconditional relationship. *Unconditional* means not pertaining to conditions, to circumstances liable to change. Since all circumstances change, as all form is ephemeral, the only truly unconditional relationship is through the oneness of formless awareness. This realization of the essential consciousness of another, of the underlying self through another, is in itself an awakening of consciousness. This is what we call love, in its truest sense. To love someone, truly, is to see them unconditionally, and so to experience union. In love, the underlying consciousness that we are awakens to itself through more than one form.

Love, this underlying awareness of oneness, can move others toward self-awareness too. When we see others deeply, we often put them at ease and give them the space to see themselves more naturally. So the light of awareness in you can awaken, to an extent, the light of awareness in another. As consciousness is more fundamental than forms, it can pass between them, and people tend to gravitate unknowingly toward people in whom consciousness is more realized. We can awaken consciousness in others by listening actively, by speaking from the heart, by hands-on healing, or simply by being present. As you observe the essential nature in yourself and others, there is space within you for unconditional acceptance of all the particularities and potential burdens of entanglement.

That said, while everyone is, ultimately, oneness, through some people consciousness is so densely or violently entangled that you may choose not to be around them. Although you can sense unity in beings, you are not personally responsible for the awakening of consciousness in others. Love and codependency are not the same. You can love someone, recognizing their essential nature, and still distance yourself from them as they act, perhaps violently, out of entangled confusion. How much you want to be a part of another person's awakening is up to you.

Although we are the same ground of consciousness, we are also distinct focal points of that one ground. So there is oneness through multiplicity—undivided awareness experiencing itself through infinite perspectives and vantage points, through all the forms of the universe. These focal points are creations of undivided awareness that serve as vehicles for its self-realization. But on a relative level they are distinct from one another, separate. So you will live as a human in one body, one form. You can realize the universality of your underlying self, but you will still experience that undivided self, at least during this human life, through one form and not another. Just because you realize that your ultimate nature transcends your personal form does not allow you to choose a different body or become another person. You cannot decide tomorrow to swap your body for another.

undividing

Nor can you decide to swap your inner burden for another.

While we are all connected, we also each live out the consequences of inner entanglement, the inner unawareness of our essential nature beyond form. We each have to come to inward realization personally, and we can only facilitate, not decide, the awakening of another. So there will be points where you realize that another does not seem compelled toward realization, but toward a long repetition of unconscious consequences, and that may be a sort of drudgery you choose not to be a part of.

Awakening Through Relationship

But it is also possible to share the spiritual path with another, and two beings moved to dissolve inner entanglement may drift together into awakening. So we find kinship and connection with others who sense some meaning beyond the surface order of our world, who feel that there "must be more than this" and are drawn to discover it. Such a relationship may not present itself as spiritual at first glance, but any who share some persistent and essential questioning of life will likely find themselves united more deeply in it over the years. These are the patient questions that transcend time and changing circumstances, the inward doubts that point to a dimension beyond the arc of a human life, and they anchor some of us together in the subtlest and most uncharted ways. So Pierre and Prince Andre, protagonists of Tolstoy's *War and Peace*, find themselves returning to the same central conversations over a great span of time and shifting fortune, amid the comfort and abundance of wealth and the trials of destitution, in an epic dramatization of such Platonic kinship. So we may find ourselves, amid a similar range of circumstances or a more temperate passage of time, returning with friends to the common ground of timeless awareness.

Such relationships, rooted in a dimension beyond form, transcend not only time but space, and may bring about synchronistic, acausal experiences. So two people connected in the formless may find themselves thinking of each other at the same time or feeling the same thing across a distance. Ten minutes after I wrote the previous paragraph with a particular relationship predominantly in mind, that friend sent me a message: a picture of Eckhart Tolle's *The Power of Now* in his hand, a book I have recommended for years that he had never come to read. Childhood friends, we hadn't talked for months, and we send each other only a few volleys of messages a year across hemispheres. It was highly improbable that he should send me a message within ten minutes of the contemplation of our relationship, and the only explicit consideration of it in this book. But material probability pertains to form, and not to the formless.

Such are the friendships that drift in and out of space and time, returning to intermittent glimmers of concrete connection like sea turtles surfacing for air. Other relationships may be more constant and involved, true experiments of unknotting, as friends live out all the mess of an inward process together. These are lives tightly interwoven, with all the imbalance and confusion of authentic reflection shared between them. Where both are moved to awakening, a natural sense of patience, grounded in total honesty, permeates the volatility of many shared experiences. Such relationship serves to cut through delusion as both confront distortions of perspective within and between themselves.

Where simplicity of awareness is the balance of a relationship, disruption is welcomed, as much as possible. Looking toward awakening one tries not to measure by smoothness of circumstance or by "getting along," but by sincerity and an openness to self-questioning. This approach tends to bring more tension and conflict—it's never fun to catch oneself, or be caught, in self-deception—but if both are rooted in an awareness of self beyond mind, beyond paradigm or identity, all storms pass. So two people can turn together to the ground of underlying awareness, and by the simplicity of its light, dissolve illusion.

Such are friendships interwoven in companionship that look always to its unmaking into unity. Then there are romantic relationships, in which two beings in complete interdependence look toward resolution into undivided union. So the full entanglement and inner confusion of each may play itself out in the other as both are given to projection and absorption. So both have the greatest possible freedom and security of connection by which to turn the whole weight of illusion toward the other, looking always to its dissolution. So some awakening couples may surface all their inner demons together, may stumble, may clash in their inward movement. So the fullest honesty and vulnerability—and even the vulnerability to fall temporary prey to the surfacing monsters of one's own unconscious, to lose oneself in absurdities and petty disagreements—may be given space.

If such depth of conflict is not grounded in a genuine openness in each, if it is not grounded in a central willingness to see through your own foolishness and resolve yourself into the plain truth of any matter, it will engender a toxic relationship of endless, blinding division. But where both in a couple are grounded in a felt experience of awareness beyond mind, beyond identity and belief, even the most impossible conflicts find their way into unpredictable resolution. These are entire tempests, impassable by any measure of the mind. Direct sincerity of conflict means some blinding and difficult periods where reconciliation seems impossible. But a return to presence, and a recognition that all outer conflict is a projection of entanglement within—a recognition that such earnest vulnerability is a shared path toward healing—stays one's course.

In this way a couple fights and comes together, patiently weathering confusion and always returning to an experience of inner vibrancy beyond temporarily bleak and tumultuous circumstances. Both look to move through all their eruptions of discord, finding some refuge from them underwater, as it were, in an underlying sense of self beyond form. Sometimes your partner may lose touch with that awareness and fall into unconsciousness, and you may have to look further inward, lighting the way for you both, speaking clearly and simply. Sometimes your partner may have to light the way for you. Faith in resolution, in the dissolution of chaos into meaning, is the constancy that eventually brings connection and the first olive branch. A return always to communication, always to the intention to engage and connect even where it's difficult, begins to settle things. In full resolution there is conversation and integration, the discussion of what has burst out of each, what demons have been surfaced, and how to bring them into a conscious experience of relationship to more clearly understand and recognize the real meaning of the next descent. So an awakening couple can find a sort of mutual traction and space to live out inner confusion and resolve themselves more deeply into one another, into the oneness of presence, coming always to a greater peace and contentment.

Of course, if both are not moved to awakening, toward the deepest resolution and the fullest confrontation of illusion within, such total expression between them cannot be lived, and will not always be contained by a felt sense of aliveness that transcends projections of inner callousness. Such difficulty of expression leads many couples to avoidance and a stale peace—an unconscious state of knotted inner tension or irresolution that rarely manifests itself overtly. The absence of clear conflict in relatively avoidant relationships may make them appear more functional, but, through denying explicit conflict, they unintentionally deny the possibility for complete resolution. Where there isn't a full and awakened aliveness, there is either some experience of active conflict, or there is buried dysfunction. Dysfunction either comes to light or lives in darkness.

If you are with a partner, feel out for yourself. Any couple can be a vessel for awakening when both can connect to awareness beyond mind and look together to resolve their inner confusion into that simple light.

Awakening Through Creativity, and the Volatility of Ambivalence

As you open inwardly you may at times feel a rush of creative energy. The push of awakening, like a tide, comes in ebbs and flows, organically, and cannot really be controlled. So inspiration comes on its own and may be engaged or invited, but cannot be forced. As we approach creativity through the broader perspective of spiritual awakening, the product—the form manifested through creative action—is of secondary value. The real meaning of creativity is union: as inspiration moves through us, it takes us imperceptibly into itself. As undivided consciousness moves through us into tangible form, we are consumed by oneness. This is the flow state we experience when we're "in the zone." In such a state there's no sense of time, but a sort of buzz, or liveliness, as we experience undivided awareness move in us. In a heightened state of presence, form is manifested through us: we create.

Where creative expression is so natural, coming of its own accord, its material fruit is inspired and meaningful, because it comes from beyond our personal intentions. So we, as individuals, as the apparent creators, take a secondary role in creation. The real expression is that of oneness, as inspiration is a push from beyond. The artist is more of an assistant to the true creator, choosing formal details—colors, shapes, words, sounds, angles, light, and so on—but not the content itself. So the artist is, for a time, possessed by a greater force and uses her mind and faculties to serve it. A sort of frenzy may ensue as she is consumed by a movement of energy and struggles to translate it formally, to get it right, as she measures whether the essential content has been appropriately rendered.

This can be a profoundly satisfying experience, as one feels oneself taken into deeper meaning, becoming a symbol for its physical manifestation. In surrender to the act of creation one feels union, total purpose, and in such connectedness the universe makes sense, is known. But it can also be a disturbing experience, frenetic and maddening, especially when excessive importance is given to the product. Where the artist feels deeply the creative impulse, but is also very invested in its formal details—perhaps in perfectionism or an outcome—there is often a volatile creativity born of ambivalence. In such a state the artist has one foot in the underlying self and the other firmly in the world. The artist may feel authentically moved, but also invested in the product or its impact, or in the perceptions of others. She may be invested in success, failure, or fame. So she vacillates between one sense of self and another. Really, this is just another, more tempestuous version of the no man's land between thought-orientation and being-orientation, between the world and eternity, often experienced during the maturation of spiritual awakening.

Such a state of volatility may be observed as manic or imbalanced. Perhaps when the artist loses contact with that deeper sense of creative meaning, shifting her center again to thoughts and social constructs, there may even be a sort of depression of disconnection and confusion. This bipolarity may be so exhausting that the sense of meaning inherent to creativity may itself be doubted, making resolution into it and the crossing of this stormy, inner landscape even more difficult. Unfortunately, in an unconscious world, few will understand this torment as a struggle toward spiritual awakening, and most (often even the artist herself) will try to bring the artist back into ordered thought-orientation, tempering the creative union toward which she is oriented. This will only prolong her ambivalence and keep her from crossing through this tempestuous state, toward integration and resolution. So the labor pains of awakening are mistaken for common pains, and the desperate efforts of inward birthing are misunderstood or ignored.

The only way through it is through it, and what is needed is courage, context, and support. The only way through it is to internally disinvest from the forms of the world, from products, impact, and material consequences, making a choice toward resolution into the formless, the heart of creativity. If you find yourself amid such torment, let yourself be dissolved by creativity, be molded by its energy as abstractly as you mold the materials of a medium: soften to it. When you fully yield to creative expression, the tension of its frenzy abates, and when you fully surrender to awakening, the volatility of its process softens.

Often artists seem to flail in their search for meaning and resolution, and for many the noise of fame only amplifies their confusion. Art, by its very nature spiritual and material, lends itself to such irresolution. The professional artist must satisfy both deepest impulse and patron, must be faithful to authenticity and to fans, must disinvest from form to express from spirit while honing and selling material works and making a name. So it is easy for the artist to feel split between two masters, form and formlessness.

Of course, this dichotomy is not ultimately necessary or always the case, as one who disinvests from form and grounds oneself deeply in awareness will often still be moved to create. Such resolved creation will ultimately be more balanced, more potent and meaningful. But it will not follow studio timetables or care much for consequences. Such deep resolution requires faith and fidelity, a constancy of purpose toward the integration of one's whole world, inner and material, into awareness, as this no man's land is crossed.

undividing

Such conflict is not uncommon, and the tortured genius is a known, and often romanticized, archetype or stereotype. The etymological origin of *genius*, from Latin, is "tutelary or moral spirit" or "generative power," perhaps first pointing to transcendent inspiration or expression. But the simple essence of genius, of creation from the undivided self, is in all of us and doesn't have to express itself so dramatically.

We all create in one way or another, whether through cooking, gardening, making our homes, staging and taking photographs, styling our appearances, planning trips, molding businesses, coming up with new ideas, envisioning future possibilities, or even through physical movement and the spontaneity of play. Creativity is so inherent to us that it is hidden throughout the fabric of our daily lives, whether or not we notice it. Often a focus on the product or result overshadows the act of creation, and the act itself is ignored. What would it be to instead look into creative energy itself, letting the product be a secondary focus, a sort of byproduct?

Where you feel moved to create, do so. Allow inspiration to move in you, to take you into it. It is, like love or meditation, a way in which we can integrate into awareness. Where anxiety or neurosis come into the creative experience, disengage from the outcome, from thoughts and structure, allowing undivided awareness to take you into it and express as it will. In your very creativity express anxiety, express neurosis, or whatever comes into the picture, allowing it all to be. As they say, "trust the process." With practice and the release of ideas or attachment to outcome, you may come almost to forget about the product, the created form, and simply enjoy the union and depth of creativity. So creativity

connection

is first meditation, secondarily craft, and you float on the waters of awakening as its tide rises through you into kinetic expression and, as it recedes, takes you more deeply into the openness of its potentiality and restful presence.

UNDIVIDING

East and West

The largest religious and spiritual traditions of our world might broadly be grouped into those of East and West, Oriental and Occidental. They often seem to send conflicting messages, with Western, Abrahamic religions directed toward God, or a god, and most Eastern religions atheistic or polytheistic. But at the core all traditions point to the same central meaning.

In the East, spirituality has often been explored through negations, while in the West it has often been approached through affirmations. For example, through Buddhism we have looked to what we are not, to the ultimate emptiness, or lack of self-nature, in forms. So the ephemeral nature of all form has been contemplated, the illusory nature of apparently solid matter. So we have seen that we are not this, not that, and that ultimately there is no fixed self. So Taoism has taught that "the tao that can be told is not the eternal tao," and "practice not-doing and everything will fall into place."

By contrast, through Christianity and Islam we have

looked to what we are, to the eternity of simplicity in the spirit. So we have looked to foundational virtues of faith in the transcendent, of giving, of compassion, and even of martyrdom. So we have been directed always to give up investment in myriad forms and seek refuge in the vast and singular intelligence of the formless, seeing it in all things. So Judaism has looked toward the deepest understanding of the world through knowledge, wisdom, and the perception of truth that transcends reason; so we have looked to the formless within the depths of form.

So the East has generally approached awakening through an eye to the impermanence of form, and the West through an eye to the constancy of the formless. "Blessed are the meek" may be another way of saying *liberated are those who see that all form lacks self-nature*. Both point to the same realization.

ORIGAMI AND UNFOLDING

If everything is the same essential awareness, why do we live in an apparently material world with clear patterns and limits?

It is clear that our surface experience of the world works in certain ways. What is hard is hard, we can't walk through walls, an object at rest stays at rest unless acted upon by an unbalanced force, and so on. Obviously the world is quite solid and material and not some vague and hazy oneness. Even though our understanding of material reality seems to break down at a small or large enough level, and quarks and dark matter defy contemporary understanding, on a cruder plane of observation the patterns described by Newton are consistent. We can go about our day expecting general continuity of experience and predictable physical patterns: things hold their shapes, and the things we design according to our knowledge of these patterns generally work. Electricity powers, skyscrapers stand, and airplanes fly.

Even where we see an apparent break in these patterns—a couple centuries ago there were no airplanes, and probably few would have believed that we could line hundreds of people into metal tubes with static wings, gliding to the other side of the world in less than a day—we understand that it is due to scientific knowledge rather than magic. We gather that someone has understood natural patterns more precisely than we do and has based this new technology on material relationships whose subtlety escapes our understanding. So even before the incomprehensible or unbelievable, we recognize that the materiality of our world is generally consistent and physical laws constant.

How is it then that, inwardly, we may come to a different sense of the universe? Many who don't pay much attention to their inner state might believe spiritual awakening to be a physical illusion, an experience rooted in the brain that only *presents* itself convincingly as transcendent. Given today's dominant empiricist worldview, rooted in sense-perceptions and their rational extrapolations, that is an understandable theory. In an age of unprecedented material manipulation, we have come to rely on the consistency of material patterns, and many don't know to look further. Yet a deeper awareness reveals what is almost another dimension, as coherent in its structure as the world's materiality. It is not just an experience of transcendence, but a kind of inward revelation by the

undividing

light of which all other experience, even sensorial experience, is secondary.

And yet this "revelation" does not stand in contrast to the world, to materiality, or to science. It is not that one is true and the other false. In the context of such awareness, reason and the sense-perceptions remain valid sources of understanding, within a relative domain. So an awakened engineer will still design by the dictates of physics. She may experience a state of awareness guiding her activity, but will still translate such inspiration through a knowledge of material patterns, respecting their demands. It is not that materiality ceases to exist in a state of awareness, but that it is intimately perceived as a feature or manifestation of essential unity. Awakening does not mean a rejection of knowledge but a deeper orientation for it.

Some myths refer to the image of a story woven in fabric. On the face of the woven fabric, there is clear form, delineation, and color. There are shapes and meaning that satisfy mental understanding. So, metaphorically, there is materiality. On the other side of the fabric there is the unmanifest—the unfinished ends of threads that blend together as an ambiguous and abstract sheet. One side is finished, while the other reveals process, and in that sense, possibility. This is not a perfect metaphor, in that the unmanifest as perceived through inner observation is not really ambiguous or abstract, but it does defy mental understanding.

When we see only the finished side of the fabric, we don't see its back end, its open process. When we only see materiality, we do not see its roots in spirit. When we are caught up in form, we are ignorant of the formless. When we are thoroughly invested in thought and reason, we cannot sense being. Where there is tension, there is not release. And yet, paradoxically, the two sides of the fabric are also one. Whether we realize it or not, there is no material without spirit, no matter without space. Material is in spirit, and spirit in material. Matter is in space, and space in matter. Form and formlessness are two sides of the same coin, of the same fabric.

So you cannot reject materiality without inadvertently rejecting a full understanding of spirit, cannot reject spirituality without inadvertently rejecting a full understanding of matter. That is probably why both visions of reality, material and spiritual, have always existed in our world. Both are persistent throughout our history, but they often find themselves in direct opposition to one another. To the "materialist," the "spiritualist" perspective is vague and unfounded; to the "spiritualist," the "materialist" perspective is superficial and myopic. But this antagonism reflects a lack of integration and is not fundamental to reality. After all, reality is one—cohesive—and the very notion of full understanding suggests the resolution of contradictions into a sensible whole.

Another illustration that may serve to elucidate the relationship between space and form, oneness and multiplicity, is that of origami. Imagine that a vast sheet, of endless length and width, lies on a flat surface. The sheet is grabbed and pulled upward from one point, from which it drapes down like a mountain. Then, that peak is turned in on itself into folds and pulled up further so more folds can be made. First there are rough shapes, abstract vistas. Soon there are galaxies, stars, and planets, one of them Earth. There, there are forests and plains, oceans and rivers, clouds and

undividing

icebergs, animals and people. Then there are crafts, carts, homes and markets, temples and courthouses, streets and entire cities, longships and castles, factories and offices, cars and airplanes, landfills and skyscrapers. The whole universe and all its forms are folded in minute detail, drawn into increasing complexity as each new fold is made.

There is such nuance of form, such a convincing and diverse world of folds, that the original sheet has practically disappeared. Few looking into this sophisticated, ordered world of endless forms, of worlds within worlds of detailed expression, would consider that such multiplicity could have some underlying unity. Yet forms are sheet, and sheet is forms. Even amid such complexity, where any form is loosened from its tight folds, it begins to reveal the singular sheet. And if the sheet is pulled on all sides away from its concentration of forms, they collapse swiftly and calamitously into oneness, and the illusion or condition of form is resolved into its underlying nature of undivided simplicity.

UNCHAINING CAUSALITY

In the West we have become accustomed to a certain perspective regarding the relationship of forms: that of causality. We have come to believe that the world is moving forward in time, that tomorrow is a new day, and that each phenomenon is brought about by causes. It is as though billiard balls hit one another, impelling a chain sequence of events. Somewhere in the mix is free will, able to act on matter and affect the future based on better understanding of, and interaction with, such causal chains.

So if we were to ask, for example, "why is there that deep quiet on a snowy day," the answer might be, "because sound waves are absorbed by porous snow." That reflects a certain truth, but the idea of causal relationship is a misperception. From a deeper perspective, there is not causality, but one, collective unfolding, the awakening of consciousness through patterned form.

As the endless sheet of origami unfolds, with the movement of each crease pushing and affecting nearby creases, so the universe unfolds. It may seem that one crease unfolds because of another, and on a relative level, this is true—the opening of one part acts upon another in a sort of chain reaction—but from the perspective of the whole, there is no chain reaction. There is instead a vast network of patterned, interrelated unfolding, the movement of each minuscule crease acting on others in predictable ways, yet ultimately compelled by the simple tendency of the entire sheet. So there is patterned relationship of activity, but not true causality.

With a clear view of the whole, the next movements of form are relatively predictable, even while they may be infinitely complex, because they always follow the tendency of the entire sheet. That said, from within the minute forms of the sheet itself the future is inscrutable, because the complexity of shapes blocks the entire process and its underlying folds from view. And yet, should the sheet recognize itself as such, even amid all its folds, the general tendency toward its total unfolding would be clear. Likewise, all the movement of interrelated activity, of minute fold against fold and apparent chain reaction, would be understood in its essence as a simple movement of the entire sheet. Just as the origami sheet might realize itself as the essential movement underlying all the activity of its interrelated creases, when you realize the profundity of what you are, you perceive that the awakening impulse in you—deepening awareness of awareness—is itself the essential movement underlying all the activity of the universe.

So a better answer to the question, "why is there that deep quiet on a snowy day" would be, "because it is so" or "because consciousness unfolds," with the addition, "the most evident interrelated conditions that give rise to such a phenomenon are the structure of sound waves and the porous nature of snow, the porous nature of snow absorbing sound waves." A better question would be, "what is the relationship between such quiet and a snowy day?" Should we come to normalize a vision of interrelated conditions rather than causality, the answer would, of course, be shorter. But the longer answer better illustrates a subtle paradigm shift away from causal chains and to a more clear image of reality: that of an unfolding self-awakening.

And yet, such a clear image of unfolding is itself a simplification, and awakening is more than the collapse of form into formlessness. Form and formlessness are not opposites, but complements. The destruction of complex form does not in itself bring about awareness. Rather, a greater complexity of form compels a deeper awareness of unity. The awakening of consciousness is a symphonic movement of form and formlessness, an undulating unfolding into enfolding, and enfolding into unfolding—an interplay of flexed creation and inactive reflection.

In any event, no amount of questioning will ever get to the bottom of things, because there is no bottom of things, nor top, nor sides. There is just groundless, undivided awareness and an enfolding unfolding of its infinitely interrelated conditional features. Through questioning we can come to better understand the interrelationship of those conditions but will never find a first cause, or base. That is because there is no base other than that baseless base hiding in plain sight: the beginningless awareness that we are.

To contemplate the interrelationship of all form can help us to disengage from unconscious paradigms. To see that all occurrences are only minutiae of a vast movement of interconnected activity, that every happening depends on so many unseen others, puts into perspective even the patterns of our own suffering. All the difficult things we experience, whether hurricanes or violent movements of human unconsciousness—crime or war, or even petty meanness—are like so many origami folds begetting and reinforcing one another perpetually. Yet every fold is also the sheet. When we see the endless interrelationship of form, it is easier to see it as endlessly impersonal and look past it into the deeper intelligence of our formless nature. Likewise, the infinite interconnectedness of a forest or solar system evokes wonder at the harmony beyond it. So it is not even essential to understand, but only to look within.

Undividing Knowledge

Today our species has a vaster breadth of knowledge than ever before. Our efforts toward specialization have been fruitful, to say the least, and we continue to understand our universe in more precise detail. Emerging knowledge and technological creations continue to surprise us, and some of these creations even move the human spirit by their audacity as we surpass ourselves, opening new worlds and defying the impossible. But knowledge and technologies alone, the tools of humanity, do not make utopias. The impact of any tool depends on its use, and unclear or unwise intentions make any tool a wrecking ball.

On a collective scale, our intentions are certainly unclear. The subtle dysfunction in each of us is magnified by our number, and our inner disconnectedness makes up an aimless and impatient whole. If we turn back toward ourselves, toward awareness, that collective character will change, and our knowledge will be put to different use. When we stop prioritizing expansionism and increasing knowledge—or quantity—and instead prioritize simple awareness—or quality—there will be a synthesis and integration of so many brilliant but disparate pieces. If our common purpose is oriented toward clarity of conscience and self-discovery, knowledge will come to ground itself in meaning. Then there will be a true human flowering.

Rather than an expansive push toward further differentiation, what would an inward movement toward synthesis and integration look like? So we've gone out to work and amassed a great material fortune of knowledge and goods. But now it crowds our home, and we live, like hoarders, amid overgrowth. What would it look like to collectively reflect, to prioritize, to choose? To take the best of our gains and set aside the rest, choosing quality over quantity?

Such a shift would move societies toward art, conscience, and spirituality. Many of our activities would—like art, counseling, organic farming, or sustainable technology—

point inward. Rather than productive quantity, true quality of life would be our collective focus. So we would continue to use the best of our technological innovations, but let go of a lot. We might let go of many complex trade routes and material spectacles. Turning inward on a collective scale may turn each of us away from the inadvertent monoculture of globalization and toward our local communities. So we may begin to source locally as much material and food as possible, relating more directly to the natural world around us.

That is not to say that the expansive movement would stop altogether. Any extreme or fundamental rejection of expansionism would be just as damaging as our current extreme of endless growth and would likely bring about social collapse. Just as we make art, go to therapy, practice yoga, visit nature reserves and public parks, and may even join monasteries in today's expansive world, so technological innovation and mass production would still exist in a synthesizing world. We might still have a global market for everything we value that cannot be sourced locally. An inward movement does not represent an absolute, just a shift in polarity, in priority.

If it were the fruit of a conscious shift in our species, such a synthesizing world would probably not choose to suffer greater pain or discomfort than we do now, nor reject technology. The same fundamental material standards that we have now would likely be maintained. As a recovering hoarder should not empty his house, should not throw away anything of real value (despite the fact that the initial discernment process is very difficult for him and may bring him to panic), nor would a synthesizing world abandon advanced technologies. But the extra and excessive would be let go. So we might keep the best and give up much of the rest.

Of course, such a process of synthesis and discernment is complex, and, as our world is so interconnected, it would be nearly impossible to let go of one part without affecting so many others. It may seem hubristic to think that one can know what is of value and what isn't, when many significant inventions have depended on apparently trivial precursors, and many useful products depend on the availability of materials generated through the consumption of less necessary goods. That is why this process of synthesis would be as collectively demanding as our expansionist movement and depend on the involvement of everyone.

Such a shift in emphasis would invigorate and reform almost every field of thought, as in all things the image of an integrated whole would become primary and the specialization of parts secondary. So all fragments would look to find their place in a deeper unity. Most fields would come to seek minimal intervention for the greatest benefit of the whole.

As we reflect on human development, we can see that our greatest inventions have freed us from pain and significant discomfort, or brought us into broader connectedness. The universal image of paradise may be a sustainable freedom from pain and discomfort, and a sustainable presence of connectedness, joy, and meaning. In the short term, freedom from pain and significant discomfort relies on the use of technologies and tools, many of which already exist, while the presence of connectedness, joy, and meaning is ultimately found in communal experience of the simplest awareness within us.

The technological question, then, is how can we create the most sophisticated instruments that interrupt life as little as possible? Can we aim for a targeted minimalism that allows us the greatest freedom of communal inward experience, free from pain and great material discomfort? Of course, the realization of such a utopia is impossible if not symptomatic of a shift in collective consciousness. Humans estranged from the vibrancy of inner awareness, with fewer structured obligations (more free time), might instead find themselves adrift in dysfunctional unconscious patterns, from petty conflict and drama to addictive and numbing activities. As the saying goes, "the idle mind is the devil's playground." But that is only true of the unconsciously idle mind, alienated from its essential nature. What about the idle mind awakened? What is a vision of humanity with its tools integrated in wisdom, a vision of the real possibility of utopia?

Architecture might look to interrupt the undivided expanse of the natural world, and our integration with it, as little as possible. We might live like pre-agrarian societies, our homes invisibly nested into nature and our neighborhoods pristine forests and prairies, with the addition of some sustainable technologies that keep cleanliness, temperature control, practical appliances, and communicative technologies up to the highest contemporary standards. Materials might be sourced locally, so each region of the world may begin to return to its unique character.

Farming might reform itself around minimal effort and intervention, largely allowing the natural processes of plants to fertilize each other, as described in Masanobu Fukuoka's *The One-Straw Revolution.* Perhaps food cultivation would also be a generally local activity, as we already see in so many community gardens. The bulk of crops might be grown with the seasons, while many others might be grown in local greenhouses, so cuisines might again begin to take on more local flavor. Permaculture, homesteading, and other movements already practice these principles.

Education might direct its primary focus to self-awareness and self-directed study, learning motivated mostly by a sense of connectedness and inspiration rather than by external prompts or structured obligation. Such an approach is already observed in many Montessori and Waldorf schools, and much of the unschooling movement. Meditation and inward awareness might be fundamental pillars of learning. Harmony and cooperation, rather than competitive models, might be favored.

Medicine might direct its primary focus to encouraging holistic health and preventative care, minimizing the need for extreme physical intervention. Awareness exercises like Qi Gong, Tai Chi, and yoga may be part of our collective understanding of health, as might intuitive herbalism. The body might be seen as an organism rather than a machine, an intelligent whole rather than an aggregate of inert parts. Integrative approaches without a mind-body division may be favored, with "alternative," Eastern, and preventative Western medicine forming a baseline of care, and invasive procedures prepared to intervene when necessary.

Psychology may come to perceive its primary purpose as the holding of a state of presence, of awareness itself. It may look to the maturation of conscious awakening in the patient as the final resolution of mental illness and disintegration. It might look secondarily to detailed knowledge compiled through empirical study and primarily to the greater intelligence of the formless, of active presence and compassion, of intuition and connectedness.

Art may look more to symbolic form than to conceptual form, using media to guide, multidimensionally, our inward movement. The artist might experience himself as a spiritual explorer, testing waters and playing out his discoveries through manifold forms. So we might find ourselves amid many intuitive maps of awakening, mythologies, and sacred symbols.

In all fields, simplicity, connectedness, and intuition might lead our activity. These examples are not intended as determined visions, but as a concrete image of some ways that a shift toward inward orientation might reshape our world. Yet the impacts of the deepest awakening of consciousness are perhaps inconceivable, since such a shift would have collective creative power far greater than any one mind can predict.

In many progressive circles this orientation is already being explored, and none of these ideas are new. But considered together they point to the possibility of tangible resolution on a global scale and give conceivable form to our deeper calling. Still, they are meaningless if considered as ends in themselves, and they can only emerge fully and fruitfully as the outer manifestations of deepening awareness. If we are to come into such an era of integration, it will happen naturally as a reflection of greater consciousness in each of us, and not through a fixation on forms.

undividing

BEYOND METHOD OR RELIGION

As nature cannot really be owned, which becomes increasingly clear as environmental destruction endangers us all, so spirituality cannot be owned. No religion, philosophy, or method can lay claim to what's within, though they can direct us toward it, and many religions have centuries of inward focus and resources supporting self-discovery. These include particular meditation and breathing techniques, detailed knowledge of significant rites of passage—including birth, reconciliation of error, individuation, death, and mourning—and many works of symbolic and sacred art. All of these can be supports for awakening if they do not become ends in themselves—idols that crowd out the meaning to which they point. We may come to see that all inward focus signals the same essential realization, the deepest of common resources, and that many of the material products of these collective endeavors are perhaps our most fundamental shared human heritage.

Already in some highly developed areas of our world, antiquated religious structures are appreciated as a cultural heritage divorced from their original doctrine. As religions have been power structures and authorities of social order as well as guides to awakening, serving both an outer, or exoteric, and inner, or esoteric, function in societies, it makes sense to let go of harsh vestiges of power. But the spiritual dimension of religions can still ground us, giving us a context to stay the course of awakening.

While such structures can contextualize or guide deepening awareness, they are not themselves that awareness. Be attentive not to confuse guide for discovery or map for destination. A doctrine may be comforting, but it is not awakening. Do not be satisfied by anything except the direct experience of awareness. There is no transformation or significant meaning in believing in spiritual depth or learning about it conceptually. The only way to understand what it's really all about is to take the cue from so many pointers, and find out for yourself.

To do so does not ask for complex knowledge and is not dependent on any method: to master a technique is not to know oneself. Awakening is not a foreign action that comes from outside of you. It starts with inward observation and the continued intention to know yourself more essentially. While such observation does give way to new and inconceivable worlds of experience, it all stems from a simple effort. Look always within, letting all forms take a secondary place in your attention, and the experience of awareness itself come to take a gentle, primary focus. Feel out presence in all things, coming to know the world through its essence, your essence.

THE INFINITE SPHERE

If our species is a vehicle for the self-realization of consciousness, where is the heart, or center, of such awareness?

In deep meditation one can come to perceive an infinite sphere—an endless funnel, a flower blooming ceaselessly out of itself. Looking into it one perceives pure awareness, divinity. It is the center of all our aims and evolution's timeless end. Therein is the heart of silence, of rest, of vibrancy and oneness. Looking into that heart, consciousness blooms through us, as us. As first expressed in the medieval *Book of the 24 Philosophers* and later echoed by seventeenth century mathematician Blaise Pascal in his *Pensées*, "God is an infinite sphere, whose center is everywhere and whose circumference is nowhere."

Human Development and the Infinite Sphere

An infinite sphere, or funnel, is a useful shape for understanding human development and its ultimate movement into awakening.

In early human societies we tend to see a greater presence of mythology, of magic and mysticism, and of some sense of universal meaning. Nomadic societies had far less control over their environments, and material conditions were harsher. Discomfort was a fact of life, and, largely due to high infant mortality rates, overall life expectancies were shorter. Yet there was more recourse to intuition and community, more free time (and, of course, freedom of movement), and more contact with nature. Some of these societies were relatively peaceful and others bellicose. A sense of community may just as well have been a crude order of tribal justice, and mythology may have mandated ritual warfare. General social orders seem to have more closely resembled a human family in their close contact, in their intimacy and discord. Humanity did not perceive itself as separate from nature, although it did generally find itself subject to nature, and much worship was directed toward the natural world and the hope for its benevolence.

The rise of agriculture brings about new societies. Control of the land comes with control of a social hierarchy, and agrarian structures give rise to property ownership. This is the general feudal system, with agrarian structures offering more surplus and development, and bringing more defined social order. Shared mythology, such as oral storytelling, gives way to some level of organized religion, doctrinal dispute, and refinement. Technologies flourish, trade routes expand, ideas are shared. There is greater organization and greater investment in order, reason, and thought. With more complexity and differentiation, distinctions tend to become clearer and better defined. Social roles are more specialized and become more clearly partitioned from one another. There continues to be a collective inward gaze, but it is more regulated and less immediate. Magic becomes theology, and spiritual practice is mediated through defined conventions and rigid hierarchies. There is greater comfort for the privileged few while many find themselves obligated, through serfship or slavery, to the regular labor of farming. More concentrated populations, more trade, and a limited diet (due to a dependence on agricultural staples), among other factors, mean disease, malnutrition, and starvation are more pervasive than they had been in nomadic societies. Humanity perceives itself as more separate from nature and often does its best to distance itself from nature.

The Scientific Revolution and Age of Reason, and the later application of their methods and discoveries through technological innovation and industrialization, bring new social orders, still more refined and specialized. The serf becomes the citizen; ideals of equality and human rights proliferate. Religion remains a powerful force, but secular philosophies are introduced, and empiricism replaces magic, mysticism, and theology as the dominant paradigm. The mind and senses alone are agreed upon as certainly real, and there is greater distance from the collective attempt at inner discernment expressed in much of theology's questioning. Inward observation becomes more subjective and personal, and collective agreements come to be based on some blend of subjective perspective and theory—mental extrapolation of sensorial observations. So all talk of reality comes to resort to reason and sense perceptions, or to opinion and belief, and experts and popular leaders generally replace figures of proclaimed inward authority. By increasingly detailed study and material observation, the surfaces of our environments are explored and catalogued in greater precision, enabling their parsing into parts and their reconfiguration into innumerable technologies. A stable food supply, modern medicine, and material comfort come to extend to a broad population while this new power of the majority gives rise to a class of marginalized minorities—those not represented by the dominant paradigm.

It has been suggested that those of us in the most developed societies find ourselves amid a new, postindustrial order, still further specialized. Theoretical knowledge is central, and, through globalization and automation, technologies replace many agricultural and manufacturing jobs. Labor shifts toward information and services, including professional and helping jobs in retail, health care, education, science, and engineering. Class structure forms around educational and technical expertise, and for this reason this order has also been called a "technocracy." "Postmodern," or even "post-truth," thought comes to distrust any universal or absolute narrative, and the subjectivity and relativism of the industrial society are amplified. A sort of particularized "realism" comes into focus, in which each segment of reality is studied in itself, with decreasing focus on a unifying ideal or principle. The explosive accumulation of information that began in the Age of Reason looks to ever greater levels of precision and detail, and in this age of information we have unprecedented control over our environments by which to ease our conditions and accommodate our circumstances, even while economic inequality and exploitation make those conditions highly uneven among us.

Of course, this is a concise and imperfect simplification of all of human history, and, like anything organic, this trajectory hasn't happened in delineated stages but as a continuous tendency. Societies move toward greater development and specialization at different rates, and in very different forms, often playing out several of these developmental threads simultaneously. But the general movement toward differentiation and mind-dominance, and away from a shared inward center and clear sense of meaning, is universal. We can see that the most advanced societies have unparalleled material standards of living, and we can also see that they suffer collective disenchantment and a search for meaning. As we grow, we seem to be growing further from ourselves.

This appears to be a natural progression. The will toward development and growth is so universal in our species that it can't be essentially denounced or villainized. If we are now approaching significant threats of overgrowth and its ensuing confusion, it's not because of something fundamentally "evil" in our species. And while the simplest society does seem more basically connected than the most industrialized societies—to nature, to community, and to a sense of meaning—it is clear that it is still equally capable of brutality and injustice. It is also clear that many simple societies today move slowly toward development, often choosing to adopt new conveniences and some paradigms from the industrialized world. This movement toward differentiation and knowledge, toward sophistication and independence from the dictates of our environments, seems to be innate to us.

Over its history, humanity has ballooned out from a central point, billowing into increasing complexity and even losing itself in that complexity. We have collectively migrated from the center to the periphery, from principles to details, from the heart to the extremities, from vague accuracy to extraneous precision. This movement has given us great power in our world and greatly eased our material conditions, even while it has distanced us from ourselves. In a sense we have flowered, pressing, as petals, from the stem outward. And yet, for now, we only know ourselves as the tips of those petals, and we find ourselves increasingly fragile, increasingly estranged from stem and roots. Such has been our outward movement.

But there can also be inward movement. While the general thrust of human activity has been expansive and growth-oriented, we have also seen a secondary contemplative dimension. So across the world we have known mystics and healers, monasteries and spiritual seekers. So we have been moved by inspired ideals of liberty, equality, and brotherhood, and civil rights movements of the sincerest conviction and vision. So we have united in anti-war protests and calls to return to nature. Even amid expanding sophistication and differentiation there have been calls to simplicity and oneness.

Still, despite this reflective gaze and the pervasive presence of inward-looking social structures, organizations, and institutions in our world, our history has more broadly tended toward outward movement into complexity and differentiation. Despite social awakenings and movements toward unity, whether religious or humanitarian, artistic or political, we have experienced a tendency toward sophistication and alienation, and away from simplicity and community. Our identities and relationships are ever more specialized and specific, and common ground recedes from view.

As this tendency toward development and expansionism, alienation and disconnectedness progresses, it will come to reach a limit, and we can already sense and see this happening. There is an increasingly tenuous trust in authority, whether secular or spiritual, political or religious. In our day, even science is distrusted amid a slew of conflicting narratives and propaganda, and the collective grounding in empiricism, in agreement based in logic and sense observation, is called into question. A new, even more alienated and fragmented paradigm may be emerging, to find new footing in a more cynical and superficial order.

Public trust can only break down so far before we find ourselves so disconnected as to provoke intuitive reaction. Especially as our earth becomes less habitable and the threat of self-annihilation through war continues to increase, there will come a point where the extreme of this outer movement toward fragmentation and differentiation will take its place in our collective awareness as clearly excessive and absurd. If the conflicts compelled by technologically-amplified fragmentation and inward alienation reach a fever pitch, they will bring collective confusion and a collapse of trust in external authority or social structure. Such a collapse might compel an active search for meaning on an unprecedented scale and so an impulse toward inward movement, reorienting our collective sense of purpose.

Like so many false starts of inward reorientation in human history, this inward wave may not may result in total awakening, but in an outward reordering into new, more sophisticated, subtle, and disconnected social structures, relative dystopias of greater material "quality of life" and inner alienation. But at some point, even an organized and relatively functioning society, by its disconnectedness, by its lack of meaning, by its reasoned insanity, will compel collective disillusionment, and the consciousness expressing itself through humanity will begin to awaken from its confused investment in form.

This inward movement does not bring us back into previous social orders, but represents something entirely new. It appears that the evolution of consciousness through our species has needed to generate this expression of increased alienation in order to compel its own impulse to full self-awareness. We don't have to live in nostalgia for the simplicity of previous orders, but we can look to them to understand more clearly the movement toward connectedness and intuition that is asked of us now. In the same way that we can look to the harmony of the natural world to guide us into awareness of the ground of consciousness that we essentially are, we can also look to the uncomplicatedness of less developed societies. We can look to their connectedness with nature, to their art and spiritual symbolism: vestiges of societies less distanced from themselves, from the ground of consciousness, even if not fully awakened to it. Yet we are not really going back to what came before, but going back consciously, awakening to the simple awareness underlying all things, and that is new in our species. Paradoxically, through losing ourselves, we are pressed to find ourselves on an unprecedented level. The loss of innocence, the loss of an inadvertent state of relative connectedness, throws us into increasing disorder that forces us toward wisdom: the conscious return to our undivided nature. Even the growing dysfunction of our world is, on one level, a natural movement toward the awakening of consciousness.

That being so, such a path to awakening is crude and painful, and it brings extreme consequences. We are stumbling toward deeper consciousness very unconsciously. This passive path to awakening looks more like the inadvertent movements of matter—of storms and landslides, earthquakes and tides—than it does active human choice. That is because the unrealized consciousness within us, as manifest in those baser instincts out of which we have not evolved, is similarly inert and unawakened. Where consciousness has not awakened to itself, whether through humans or the natural world, it is always somehow indifferent, callous. And yet, we are not wholly inert. We are not rocks or waters. We do not need to be forced into awakening by external circumstances brought about by self-ignorance. We can come to understanding and choose to move inward. Our greater consciousness gives us the free will by which to turn our awareness more deeply upon itself, facing inner division and making light of darkness, life of apathy. We don't have to be thrown into a pit to fight our way out. When we see the "big picture," we have a choice: we can prioritize realization.

Chakras

We see spheres or funnels everywhere in the universe, from planets to stars, spiral galaxies to flowers, trees to bubbles, fruits to atoms. It is likely that the infinite sphere is a useful shape for describing human development because it is an organizing principle of the universe, central to the relationship between space and form. It may be fundamental to the way that the oneness of spacetime expresses itself through matter; such a shape seems to be at the root of the union between undivided oneness and the multiplicity of forms.

Gravity is the phenomenon responsible for shaping matter into spheres, or points, the force by which a planet or other body draws objects toward its center. But more than just a mechanical force, gravity was suggested by Einstein to be an essential characteristic of the universe, a curvature or warp in space and time caused by massive bodies. As both a curvature of spacetime and a force that draws mass into points or spheres, gravity may be as inherent to spacetime as it is to matter, bridging the apparent division between them. The sphere may be the shape through which spacetime emerges into matter, through which formlessness emerges into myriad form. Scientists today theorize that particles and antiparticles and bubbles of spacetime snap in and out of nothingness, and many believe that our universe expanded rapidly from a small dot that emerged from nothingness.

Planets, bubbles, trees, particles—so we perceive funnels or spheres without, with our sense perceptions, but for us there are more significant manifestations of the infinite sphere within. As we look inward, we may come to perceive that our awareness is rooted in endless funnels, or infinite flowers, within. In the Hindu tradition these endless funnels have been referred to as the chakras. The experience of the chakras is as direct as that of your sense-perceptions and is most like the experience of the body. So you can close your eyes and sense your arms, sense your legs, sense your head. You don't need to be looking at them to feel that they are there. The chakras may come to be felt in the same way, through inner awareness.

There is no need to believe in them or to try to understand them theoretically. As you deepen awareness, perhaps you will feel them, and perhaps you won't. It's nothing to fixate on, because fixation itself is the creation of a burden, a blockage in the chakras. Spirituality is a matter of direct experience, and getting caught up in beliefs about your inner world, as many do, only takes you into a mental and emotional fantasy that distances you from that direct experience. Reading about these interior funnels may be useful for contextualizing an experience you're already having and for getting a sense—or general "roadmap"—of what you might find looking within. But these are just words, and even a good map is only a superficial image of a real place.

In a quiet context with some "space to think," forget about your thoughts for a moment and direct your attention inward. It doesn't matter whether or not there are thoughts in your mind. They have little to do with inner observation. Look within, and feel out the experience of the body. Feel the existence of each part—from the top of the head, to the neck, to the chest, to the arms, and down to each area of the body.

Outside the mind, outside of thoughts, how do you know you exist? Can you feel that you are? This is the practice of awareness. As you continue such simple, inward focus, perhaps over minutes, hours, days, years, or decades, it will deepen. New interior forms emerge: sometimes physical aches or pains, sometimes tensions, sometimes emotions. Most such forms will slowly dissolve into your attention, into the awareness you direct toward them. But presence will remain, the experience of awareness itself. You may notice that awareness express itself through subtle but persistent inner funnels, inner flowers of consciousness.

So the chakras are infinite funnels, like energetic membranes. Here words are only approximate, since the observation of the chakras is through sensing and feeling. Their root is oneness, undivided consciousness, divinity. Their petals are the psyche. (There is no stem in this image, just an endless flower with oneness as its center.) These energetic petals of the chakras can twist and tear with trauma or other circumstances we encounter. Our inner burden consists of formations in the energetic structure of these petals, or funnels. That is to say that the complexes we subjectively experience have their central objective form in the chakras. All the accumulated weight that we carry around and any persistent emotional distress we feel—whether anxiety, anger, sadness, or depression—is the experience of a particular energetic state, a particular distortion of consciousness within.

Of course, this distortion is reflected in the body, perhaps in the nervous system and in the brain, as neuronal activity also corresponds to our inward states. But the central presence of inward disturbance is in the chakras, and in most cases the empirically observable form—the body, the nervous system, the brain—is a secondary reflection of this deeper manifestation. (Clearly, this is not always the case, as injury to the brain can directly affect personality and inner experience.) The chakras and all their distortions are the objective form of what we often refer to as the soul, and they reach from the infinite heart of awareness into the conditioned relativity of our experience.

So the knots of the psyche take place, more specifically, as distortions in the energetic membranes called the chakras. Depression, trauma, and repressed emotions exist as energetic distortions within, like twists in a magnetic field. Those distortions are, ultimately, the same undivided awareness, but they are twisted into specific form. So they have a specific quality or charge, even while they are ultimately just awareness. That charge they carry can seem to have a mind of its own as we are moved into unconscious action.

There is a sort of momentum within us of distorted awareness disintegrated from its root, and as we observe ourselves attentively, we will notice many unconscious, almost autonomous inner drives. Many of us carry heavy emotional burdens and density of past pain and suffering, all that we have had difficulty experiencing fully. These dense, energetic twists, often linked to particular thoughts and ideologies, are always active within us. We constantly act from the subconscious impulses of such disintegrated drives, usually without even realizing that we are doing so. Sometimes, these beliefs are so unconscious and disconnected that they even clash with or contradict one another, and we live with unexplored and charged ideological contradictions—beliefs and perspectives that we have not reconciled. Other times, where there is greater consciousness, we are more aware of our inner conflicts and biases but have not yet resolved them through a practice of awareness (any activity, such as meditation or counseling, that brings us into a state of reflection and presence).

When we are "triggered," when our conscious experience moves into, or is overwhelmed by, these twists, we see our-

undividing

selves overtaken by these drives as we perhaps explode in anger or collapse into panic. Then there is an acute opportunity for resolution. When these disintegrated twists are activated—when they come into our conscious experience and we start to live them out—we have the chance to heighten our awareness of them. Through patient and intent observation, the pure consciousness of observing awareness begins to dissolve this distorted consciousness into itself. The engaged neutrality of the observer takes repressed and intense emotions into itself, softening and resolving them into its simplicity.

If this sounds abstract, see for yourself. The next time you experience charged emotions, take a step back and observe them attentively, even if you continue to act them out. See if any unexpected spaciousness or healing comes through engaging that simple clarity of the observer. Invite the chaos within you into your conscious experience, and let it be. So you begin to untie inner knots. Rather than fighting with inner conflict, tightening existing knots, engage them gently, patiently. A highly focused and active practice of presence will create some space even around the tensest drives within you, and what is hard will slowly yield into the light that you are.

As we look within, connecting to presence, we experience the aliveness beyond the chakras, at their root. That whole, undivided oneness is healing. It is a balanced field of potential energy that becomes kinetic, becomes active, through our awareness of it. So engaged, it moves through us, through the chakras, and out into the world around us. So we see someone "light up" when in love or inspired. In love or inspiration we draw from formless awareness, moving it through us and into the world.

As we come into a state of quiet alertness, we move that energy of awareness through the chakras and their twists and tears. We move the balanced awareness of oneness through the distortions of the funnels of our psyche, and that energy mends the distortions, resolving them back into itself. So, through presence, the tangled distortions of the chakras, of the psyche, are resolved into oneness.

This experience can sometimes be unpleasant, disorienting, or hard. So we feel inspired or connected, and as that energy of inspiration moves through inner distortions, we suddenly experience difficult memories, activated trauma, repressed emotion. So after a new and frightening adventure the child doesn't cry until he sees his mother, that symbol of trust that opens him inwardly, letting his emotions out. So you can push yourself through a difficult experience and only feel the emotional "hangover," or physical illness, as you finally relax. So the connected touch of a partner can bring up pain or trauma within, opening us to the sometimes overwhelming experience of resolution. So creative activity can bring us suddenly into dark spaces that we express into form. So in meditation or yoga our experience may suddenly shift from a state of peace to overwhelming emotion, and we may burst into tears in the middle of a crowded studio. This is the healing process. As we look within, we bring the relative entanglement of our psyches, as manifest in the chakras, into the underlying indivision of vibrant awareness, and we experience that process.

The chakras have their roots in oneness and extend outward into the entangled distortions of all our complicated experience. Regardless of whether or not we experience the chakras, when we look inward we draw from the depths of our essential nature, of undivided awareness, and so we come to resolve all the distortions of fragmentation into it. In a quiet pause, in simple meditation, in giving ourselves space from investment in thought and circumstance, we can feel out that basic awareness directly and bring all entanglement into it. Such is the dissolution of essential ignorance and the transcendence of our human partiality. Such is the process of full self-realization as consciousness and the maturation of spiritual awakening.

As individuals, and as a collective species, we have unknowingly expressed ourselves outward, from root to petal, ensnaring ourselves in complexity. It is time we turn our gaze back to root and beyond, becoming aware of the totality of ourselves beyond form and resolving ourselves in that awareness.

Boundaries

Often in spiritual communities and communes—groups that look for meaning beyond normative societal guidelines—boundaries are confused or ignored. It is natural that in the explorative and experimental search for new structures reflective of greater meaning, existing order is lost. Often someone may come to such a community through disillusionment and dissatisfaction with the greater society and global culture that she has been a part of, seeking sincerity or healing. So she is more than willing to cast off those norms and try something new. But it is quite possible that amid the searching and shapeless landscape of many communes, the abandoned order of the broader society, despite its obvious dysfunction, starts to look more sane. The boundaries and structure of the broader society, despite their egocentric foundation, may offer order and relative "normalcy" that many communes do not. How is it that an earnest search for meaning and healing so often finds itself rootless and disjointed?

We are often driven to explore a sense of meaning in such parallel societies by a sense or experience of alienation or meaninglessness in our general culture. The strange values of many contemporary cultures drive many to look for some more earnest corner of the world. Perhaps we are driven away by their determined superficiality, their frenzied fixation on constant productivity and unmeasured growth at the expense of human connection, or their ignorance of broader consequences and sustainability amid the blinding lure of short-term gains. We may be disillusioned by a culture of quantity and look for quality. Or we may be disillusioned by injustice and apathy, by sexism, racism, homophobia or transphobia, by bigotry and entitled small-mindedness. Somehow we come to prioritize connection, meaning, the simplicity of inner freedom, and love.

So we look for some community doing things differently, some countercultural or more awakened enclave that shares our purpose. We come together in the image of connectedness and a common good. We prioritize the formless, looking only to the transcendence of our individualistic aims, as

undividing

many spiritual teachings have directed us to. We look beyond our limiting senses of order, trying to become one. We forgo personal limits and boundaries, seeking union and freedom. We are anything but "basic," anything but "square."

But something feels wrong. Perhaps personal or sexual boundaries are crossed. We stretch ourselves beyond our limits, hoping to find meaning, but instead we find some strange disturbance. We look to follow teachers or spiritual masters and are swept up into distorted hierarchies. We seek a way out of confusion and alienation and may find ourselves more alienated and confused than before. What looked like liberty proves to be libertine. It is as though we have endeavored to stare into the sun—the unlimited light of formlessness, beyond boundary and structure—and ended up blind.

There is the formless, and there is form. There is spirit, and there is material. The base of our universe may be infinite space and time, but it expresses itself in a panoply of consistently ordered matter. Just as all things have their roots in the formless, they also all flower into form, and every flower has its shape and season. So gravity is constant, so orbits are predictable, so weather is patterned and "ecosystems" balanced.

The realization of oneness is not in rejecting order and the world but in finding that its essential nature lies beyond its surface manifestations. So, as a parallel in the sensorially observable world, we might say that a deep scientist does not reject the appearances of matter, does not deny the existence of electrons or galaxies, but looks to understand their origin, their more essential nature beyond first appearances.

As we look to oneness, we can also look to multiplicity. There is no final binary, no contradiction between spirit and matter. So we can know that we are, essentially, one, while respecting the features of that oneness, the relative boundaries and limits inherent to our human form. While we are the universe, we are also its conditional and particular expressions, and during the time that we take such forms, we can respect their integrity. So we can respect our likes and dislikes, our preferences for comfort and physical security, our visceral sense of personal boundaries, our capacity for discernment, our innate sense of order. Within that natural sense of who and what we are as humans, we can look deeply within, beyond relativity. So we can observe the universe from the particular inner eye of our form, and our particular form from the eye of the universe.

It is worth remembering that millennia of devoted spiritual practice have taken place in monasteries, which are often contexts with very clear order, precedent, and norms. The unstructured spiritual environments we often see today are largely a product of the more secularized societies in which they form. Because the collective dictates of modern societies are so estranged from spirituality, many people find it difficult to integrate their normal sense of social structure, boundaries, and rules into an explicitly spiritual environment. This was probably less the case, for example, in Spain in the Middle Ages, when social law was integrated with and justified by Catholicism, and monastic rules were more like stricter extensions of the norms of the general society. Of course, even in such clear structures power was often abused, and such hierarchies of order, both in monasteries and in society, lent themselves to injustice. But the continuity of context between everyday life and spiritual communities probably made those communities less parallel societies, less lawless, less confusing and disorienting than many spiritual environments today.

If you join a spiritual community or participate in any spiritual context and choose to give up some normative order as you step into something new, pay clear attention to your inner sense of justice and boundaries. Spirituality is not something that comes from outside of you, but from within. While self-realization can be pointed to, it is just a deepening of what you already are and what you already know. If it feels unnatural to you, it is not spirituality. Paradoxically, any new state of awakening you experience is always more essentially familiar to you than the less connected state you had previously lived in. Trust yourself, trust your gut and your instincts. Do not get caught up in beliefs or obligations, but keep returning to the experience of what you *are*. After all, it is your own inner sense that has led you to look for more. Any real guidance should ask you to trust that inner sense first and only support you to know and enter into it more fully.

Justice

As a tree draws water and nutrients from its roots, and as the leaves on any branch will die if its structural integrity is broken, so all form reaches into the formless through its own natural structure. Justice is the structural relationship between form and the formless, between matter and space, and any clear sense of morality instinctively protects that integrity. Ideally, laws are formalizations of such natural intuition. Laws are social agreements that keep the structural integrity of form's relationship to formlessness, of the relative to the absolute, and thus keep us oriented toward genuine progress: that of self-realization.

However, as our world becomes more invested in increasing sophistication and thought, it is relatively alienated from its underlying nature as undivided awareness. So its sense of order, truth, and justice becomes self-referential, fragmented, "postmodern," and relativistic. Laws and social agreements are increasingly perceived as subjective creations, as social constructs without absolute orientation. Of course, as all forms are particular, and as all societies and individuals are unique, that is partially true. Since the particularities of each individual and society are unique, laws and social agreements do have a degree of relativity wherever they pertain to relative questions, to questions pertaining to the particularity of form. Yet multiplicity has its roots in oneness, and, in that sense, even respect for the particularity of any form requires a sense of its relationship to the formless.

So each person has a different, innate sexual orientation. Each person knows, inwardly, their gender experience. Some people are quiet and some are loud, some passionate and others easy-going. Each of us has a different cultural inheritance and character that will define the particularities of our inward path. We all have, within us, an instinctive sense of integrity and of the authentic expression of our form.

On the one hand, this is an example of relativity and "subjective" truth—each person knows the natural particularity

undividing

of his or her form expression. And yet, on the other hand, this is also an example of absolute and "objective" truth. In a universal and absolute sense, it is just to respect each form's structural relationship to the formless. So it is absolutely unjust to repress one's natural sexual orientation, experienced gender, or way of being. It is absolutely unjust to repress the genuine expression of any form, to deny the particularity of form as manifest by the formless. It does not matter what one feels about it, what one subjectively experiences, or how an entire society feels about it. What is, is. Each form, as a feature of the formless, has its natural expression.

When any of us looks patiently within, she will find there the simplicity of her essential nature as pure awareness, and such awareness will express itself wholeheartedly through the relative uniqueness of her person. So each tree draws water from the same ground but does so through a unique shape. So the center of each of us is the same everywhere of pure awareness, even while our circumference of branches reaches out into relativities, to nowhere; the center and the relativities reinforce each other in awakening, just as both root and branches make the vitality of a tree.

Amid our contemporary investment in increasing sophistication, we are, in some ways, more inclined to respect the particularities of form, largely because we are alienated from a collective sense of clear orientation or any absolute. In many cases we have greater respect for subjective expression, for the relative perspective of each person. That has, on the one hand, led to moral clarity regarding individual rights and greater acceptance of diverse form-expression. On the other hand, it blinds us to the awareness of deeper truth. In becoming entangled in the branches of diverse form and alienated from our root, we have a greater focus on each branch even as we struggle, more than ever, to recognize the whole tree and ground—to cut through overgrowth and excess to a clear sense of collective meaning.

So we are paradoxically better at defining the rights of the individual, attending to the particularity, and worse at anchoring him in a world of connectedness and genuine sustainability. So we defend the right of the individual to express the details of his authentic particularity, just as we find ourselves increasingly unable to defend him from an unchained and impersonal economic order, seemingly self-willed toward its own collapse; unable to discover a collective sense of meaning that would contain the indirect and aggregate effects of so many partial wills, of pollution and economic exploitation; unable to provide for any person or creature the deepest justice—defense from the prospect of an uninhabitable earth. We are more able to satisfy his wants and less able to understand his deepest needs. We are increasingly able to legislate for quantity, but not for quality. We struggle to orient our societies toward the heart of progress and the fulfillment of our highest aim and satisfaction, our self-realization. Meanwhile the very logic of relativism, of thought alienated from undivided awareness, can be twisted into any strange definition of truth, while the very notion of justice depends on some sense of universal truth or absolute meaning, vaguely intuited or conceptually inherited from an age of social thought less alienated from its undivided nature.

As matter relates to space in particular patterns and shape, so all material beings partake in the formless by their own particularities. The full value of any form can only be seen in the light of the formless; the full integrity of any being can only be clearly valued in the depths of sensed oneness and in love.

Privilege is a concept central to much of our current consideration of justice and might be defined as a circumstance in which the aggregate forces of ignorance seem to work in one's favor. So a collective delusion of divinely anointed royalty conferred favors on a genetic lineage, a collective delusion of racial supremacy confers favors on that race, a collective delusion of meritocracy confers favors on the successful or wealthy, a collective delusion of institutional solidity confers favors on the documented, accredited, or ordained. Where there is delusion—identification with thought and paradigm—there is alienation from the undivided self, from clear awareness of the oneness of all beings.

On the deepest level, a system of privilege is in nobody's interest, because no one benefits from a world out of touch with itself. While a partial system confers temporary favors on certain groups, such an unjust state is divided, unstable, and unsustainable. Any state of fragmentation is a state of disease, whether individual or collective.

So we can try to address all injustice and recognize every manifestation of privilege, but as long as there is essential self-ignorance within us, there will always be injustice, there will always be privilege. Until we come to self-realization, resolving inner fragmentation into undivided awareness, wherever injustice is addressed in one form it will come to take another as new unresolved paradigms breed new biases.

Today there is a lot of attention given to making more inclusive systems, and many believe that ideal justice will come through functioning systems. While these are noble intentions, they contain at their root an inherent contradiction. What we call systems are organizations of human unconsciousness. They are mechanistic structures of the mind, and, like machines, they are less conscious and responsive than organic beings. Our systems are a stand-in for consciousness; they are our best attempt to order the symptoms of our inner dysfunction without recognizing it for what it essentially is: an unrealized state of being.

Because any system is ultimately a mental configuration of human unconsciousness, it is necessarily structured as a binary. Like any machine, it will perform its allotted tasks well and ignore the reality of its immediate surroundings. On some level, any system will always be biased, always be unjust, because it is always inert. Only the full light of consciousness is supple and alive enough to respond sensibly and compassionately to the reality of its surroundings in any given moment. So we will only live in a fully just world when our need for systems dissolves into the light of the undivided awareness that we are.

Yet we can bring justice to the world when we do so from a felt sense of connectedness and love. Even as we take concrete and pragmatic steps toward change in our world, we must look within to discern the genuine and lasting content of that change. Then we may, in the most visceral sense, bring light to darkness, both within ourselves and in the world around us. Then each confrontation of injustice is itself a movement into the realization of deepest unity, a movement of the world's awakening to itself as the living indivision behind all form.

THE UNION OF FORM AND FORMLESSNESS

Oneness

If we are eternal and infinite awareness, why do we experience ourselves always through a singular focal point in space and time?

The undivided awareness that you are has invested itself into a specific feature, a focal point, but that limitation of perspective that defines, or may seem to entrap you in, personal experience is only a temporary condition of your deeper nature as pure awareness. It seems that the formless, the pure awareness that you are, invests itself into form in order to use those forms to experience itself more deeply, to more deeply awaken to itself. This is the universal significance of human existence, and, really, of all existence.

On the one hand, we experience ourselves in physical bodies in a world with material conditions. As long as we, consciousness, experience ourselves through this human form, we will have all the relative sensations conditional to a human body: pain, hunger, happiness, sadness, heat, cold, and so on. And on that relative level of experience, which is truly human experience, we are subject to all the shifting conditions of the physical body. Degeneration of the brain or nervous system, or injury to various body parts may cause a change in such human experience—we may lose our sight, motor function, or memory. Our material conditions may bring us pleasure and comfort, and some things will feel, look, sound, smell or taste good and some bad, depending on the particularity of each human form.

And yet we can come to sense that this human form is relative, not finally our true self. Just as the room or setting you're experiencing around you as you read this page is a temporary condition of your experience that will change when you leave it, so our very humanity is a temporary condition of our experience of the atemporal awareness that we most essentially are. Though you will certainly experience yourself through the conditions of a body at a single, unique focal point in space and time, you are, more essentially, the awareness that is conscious of such experience.

Ultimately, space and time are not separate, but the same. Time is a concept we derive from the motion of forms. So the earth rotates once, and we call it a day, or it revolves around the sun, and we call it a year. Or a raindrop falls to the ground, and we see it quickly shift position and disappear. Forms are not static, so we consider a dimension that accommodates their constant changes in position and call it time. We invent a useful practical distinction between space and time for our own purposes, when really there are just shifting forms in spacetime.

Even the shifting forms and spacetime are not separate. No thing exists outside space or time; all things occupy space and change over time. So spacetime is the ground of all forms, intrinsic to their existence. So forms might best be described

the union of form and formlessness

as features or expressions of spacetime.

Through constant inner attention we come to sense that awareness is also inherent to spacetime. As we awaken, disinvesting from the changing circumstances of shifting form, from the features of spacetime, our experience of awareness is not interrupted by movement through spacetime. We, ourselves features of spacetime, can travel across states or oceans, and still, when we look within and around, there is awareness. Fifty years later, still there is awareness. There is no point, amid shifting features of form, where the inner depths of awareness are interrupted (even in sleep and physical unconsciousness, there is underlying awareness), just as there is no point where spacetime is interrupted. The depths of awareness are always sensed in all things and are as continuous and infinite as spacetime. In every space, in every time, there is awareness. So we come to sense awareness not as a conditional feature of spacetime, but as spacetime itself.

Right now, in this moment, you are reading these words. Now, in this same undivided moment, you are reading different words. In the same undivided now, later, you close this book. In the same undivided moment, afterwards, you stand up. In the same undivided now, tonight, you sleep. In the same undivided now, three years later, perhaps you take a trip. In this same moment, thirty years later, circumstances have changed entirely. It is always this moment, always this undivided now.

Now, in this moment, all the infinity of forms in space are present. At this moment every person on earth exists, every building exists, every decaying form exists, all the oceans exist, every flower in the universe exists, the craters of the moon exist, emerging forms exist, the sun's heat exists, distant stars exist, unseen galaxies exist. Now, in this same moment, the entire universe has shifted its position, and many planets have shifted a thousand miles; innumerable forms have come into being, and innumerable forms have ceased to be. In the same moment, three hours later, babies have been born, flowers across the earth have opened, animals have died, and the whole universe has turned into entirely new forms. Now, in this moment, twenty years later, everyone you know takes different form, the babies are twenty years old, the earth has absorbed decaying animals; every form in the universe is different. In this same moment, twenty billion years from now, humanity is extinct, the earth is gone, the sun has died, stars are born, atoms are destroyed, molecules form, galaxies are destroyed, and galaxies are born.

Every circumstance changes; every feature of spacetime shifts. But it is always this now, always this awareness, always spacetime.

Through our human form the simple awareness of spacetime expresses itself most elementarily in the funnels of chakras, the most basic feature of our human form. They are the centers of perception by which we can turn awareness back upon itself, looking into infinity and eternity. So through us, as us, the universe observes itself, knows itself, becomes self-aware, awakens.

So in deep meditation we can sense that the undivided consciousness that we are is far more profound and fundamental than the particularity and limitation of the vantage point—always singularly defined within time and space—that describes our human experience. The limited focal point inherent to our human perspective is a manifestation, or feature, of that deeper indivision and a temporary condition of that infinite and eternal underlying reality of pure awareness that we, and all things, essentially are.

Seeing Through Inner Resistance

Even the form of all inner entanglement, all ignorance, has its roots in the formless. Looking within, recognize that—like all form—even your ignorance, even your inner burden, is a manifestation of the formless. Even your blockages are a manifestation of oneness. Look within and come to see that all heaviness or confusion is just an appearance taken on by undivided awareness, just a feature of consciousness. As you recognize the lack of any final substance to the heaviness or resistance you feel as you look within, bringing consciousness to entangled consciousness, the illusion of fixed form is broken and inner division is dissolved. This can be a continued practice of deepening resolution. By the timeless space of awareness, look intently into tension, letting it slowly shift and unmake itself into space.

Bliss in Polarity: Form and Formlessness

Why does the formless invest itself into form in order to self-awaken? What is the specific relationship between form and formlessness, and awakening?

Everywhere in the universe we can see this relationship between form and formlessness, between active expression and inactive rest. So our hearts beat systole and diastole, so we wake and sleep, so we are born and die, so with the seasons nature waxes and wanes. So all art is patterned form and space, sound and silence, movement and stillness. So all forms come into existence and cease to exist. This constant shift in polarity between form and formlessness, matter and space, kinetic and potential, action and inaction, is fundamental to reality.

Such polarity is not antagonistic, but reciprocal. So we tend to sleep more soundly after a day of activity and act more meaningfully after a night of rest. As we express the potential awareness of spacetime into kinetic action and form, there is invigoration, excitement. Looking within and observing that universal tendency toward manifestation, that systolic movement in ourselves, we can sense its nature. This is our creative impulse, our beginning, our flexed outward push. There is something healthy and expansive in this movement into form. Through inward observation we can also recognize the complementary polarity, the instinct to return to restful potentiality. This is the movement into ease and relaxation, to ending and a different sort of opening, an unflexing into inactivity. There is renewal and integration in such withdrawal and release into formlessness. In classical Chinese philosophy, these two universal poles are respectively called yang and yin.

You can observe an example of this universal polarity in your own inquisitive process. You may see the creative and expansive push in the way that you magnify thoughts or theories by writing them onto a page or screen, giving them decisive material form. Then, amid such magnification, clarity is sought. But this clarity requires an inward sense and represents the reciprocal, reflective, almost inactive polarity. Reflection does not magnify but steps back and considers, discerns, culls. Then, out of that space of consideration comes the push of a more precise question and again an

the union of form and formlessness

expansive movement. There is new magnification and new synthesis, one polarity and another, again and again. Pulsing like jellyfish, we move more and more fully into the heart of any matter through a fractal process of discovery.

So we give shape to our homes through an expansive movement of creation, bringing vague senses of preference and feeling into colorful form. That home, that concrete expression of feeling, becomes a context for living, for rest, for privacy and inward experience. As we relax into it, grounded by its containing presence, we may feel moved to repeat the process, to again express and refine further details in creative, kinetic expression and to again rest in that deepened outer context.

So we might express something difficult or unclear within, speaking earnestly to another, perhaps a friend, partner, or therapist. As we express conflicting emotions and give them form, something is liberated, and there is creation, traction, expansive opening. Then, through the new space and context we have realized, we converse, and, through the other person, a mirror of our expression allows us deepened self-observation and reflection. Amid such reflection perhaps new feelings emerge and the process is repeated, once and again, in deepening self-realization.

So, by the intelligent inspiration of the formless, we are moved to create authentic form. Through a cathartic push formlessness crystallizes into temporary form and by that acute expression, mirrors itself more deeply. By means of formal expression, we turn our awareness back on itself, becoming more deeply aware of awareness, awakening to ourselves beyond form.

So a vast body of water at once articulates itself into a

million bristling ripples, awakening its underlying stillness.

So through our species myriad spiritual texts and works of art have been manifested, conscious expressions of form to ignite the formless depths of our hearts.

So the love of form is a natural expression of the universe, but form can only truly be loved in the light of the formless. We fall ever more deeply in love with the unmanifest through the creation and adoration of its manifestations, not as ends in themselves, but as symbols of an eternity within us. So a flower blooms in full and decisive radiance, and its petals fall away as it continues to blossom endlessly out of itself.

So the universe magnifies itself through its expansive push in order to observe itself more deeply. Its expansive push is as inherent to its awakening as its reflective withdrawal. It creates and also synthesizes. But it is not finally interested in its creation, in form. Form is a means to deepening self-discovery. The universe creates and reflects through its creation, and therein is the explosive joy and vitality of its awakening. Like jumping dolphins weaving in and out of water, the unimpeded process of such creation and reflection, of expansion and contraction, is blissful, and that bliss, like a guiding harmony or frequency, evokes its own balance. As a bicyclist is guided by upright posture to keep intuitive balance between two poles, so the universe is guided by such harmonic vitality.

Expression into form is grounding, and reflection into formlessness is integrating. We can block inner health by denying either polarity, by refusing to express form that moves in us or by refusing to let go of form to which we cling. In letting go, we express more naturally, and in expressing

the union of form and formlessness

naturally, we let go. Both polarities, of creation and inactivity, make the vitality of inward balance and the fertility of presence.

Especially after trauma, there is meaning in reinforcing the interrelationship between formlessness and form. Vitality and rootedness within come from sensing our essential nature beyond form while integrating ourselves into or syncing ourselves with the patterned form-expressions of the universe. After trauma, which can seriously confuse our sense of orientation, there is a strong need to ground ourselves in pattern, in routine, in the solid and dependable, perhaps in the regularity of day and night or the regularity of the seasons. The universal impulse to ground in form-expression is why we may be moved to order our space, to sing to ourselves, or even to look in the mirror. Even in a state of dissociation after trauma, we may observe ourselves hugging our bodies, physically rocking back and forth as the intelligence within looks to integrate itself into a sense of connection and pattern—into energetic balance. So we unconsciously seek, or even fight, to reestablish the relationship between form and formlessness, between patterned universal expression and pure awareness.

We have all probably had the experience of waking up in the dark feeling eerily disoriented, especially during times of significant change. We turn on a light and suddenly perceive form. It doesn't matter what the form is or whether we are sleeping in a new place. The experience of form, of concrete reality itself, is familiar. If that's not enough to ground us, perhaps we take a walk or look to the ritual of repeated routines, whether pouring a glass of water or making a cup of tea. Then there is some fundamental gratitude for the continuity of pattern in the universe, even if it's the unyielding regularity of a city street or the muffled darkness of moonlit woods. The observation of form in its continuity, or just the abstract recognition that, even in the remotest corners of the universe, form is expressed in patterns, is reassuring. So amid disorientation we ground ourselves in form, and come back to ourselves. Form grounds, and formlessness perceives.

If we are in a state of significant imbalance, the approach toward balance may push the polarities of expression and integration, form and formlessness, toward both extremes. So if we've repressed something for a long time, denying the movement of manifestation and expression, it may explode out of us with little space for reflection. Conversely, if we've pushed ourselves into constant activity, we may burn out and collapse into a state of exhaustion, struggling to find traction in more modest activity. As denial of either pole tends to stem from the same unawareness, from being out of touch with ourselves and ignoring our natural impulses, we often find we have denied both poles simultaneously.

As you become aware of your imbalance, either because of a choice to look inward or because you are confronted by outer consequences, prioritize resolution. The fastest course to balance is acceptance of both extremes and trust in the natural intelligence of both polarities. This nature is not something you invent but a universal principle experienced within. So, like any expression of universal principle, like the natural world around us, it will find its balance when you stop interrupting it and let it be. Let yourself be moved to express what's within, even absurdly, irrationally, and let yourself collapse into inertia. Pay attention to the impulses

the union of form and formlessness

within you, and respect their guidance.

Ask yourself: how many external consequences are greater than those of denying your experience? What would it be to speak and act from a state of connectedness, from what moves you, rather than what seems to "make sense?" What is it to let loose and stop trying to control yourself, tightly monitoring what you say and how you behave? If you find yourself blocking what you truly want to do and say because it seems pointless or absurd, try opening that valve and moving into the blindness and discomfort of new experience.

Live out the disorder of inner entanglement, letting tears in the chakras bloom out into expressed form and then resting into the resolution of their deep potentiality, drawing from undivided awareness. In a constant back and forth, express outward and move inward, mending what's tangled or painful within and moving more deeply into the self. As you come into a state of deeper resolution and balance, you may find that both poles come toward a closer unity, allowing you to act and express from a restful state of awareness, uniting form and formlessness. Such is a central concept in Taoism: *wei wu wei*, meaning "action without action" or "effortless doing." Like the pressureless pressure or active inactivity required to escape a Chinese finger trap, such a state of subtle integration engages both poles simultaneously, igniting a robust clarity of presence.

This liveliness of harmonic balance is what we call health, in its fullest sense, and this is the integrity of health from which we are increasingly estranged as a species. We remain invested in the material fruits of our expansionist tendency, invested in prosperity as an end in itself and ignorant of its deeper significance as one pole in the true health of our species. We know ourselves as form but are alienated from the other side of the coin, from formlessness. We fail to see form in its full context, as a relative expression of the simple and endless aliveness that we all are.

As consciousness casts itself into increasing formal complexity in order to more fully awaken to itself, we now find ourselves at an extreme. Now we are compelled to collectively look within, realizing a magnitude of awakening that corresponds to the magnitude of our outward expansion into complexity. Unlike less conscious formal expressions of the universe that live this balance by default, we must decide to step out of all our created confusion of separative paradigms to recognize it consciously. We must, by the very consciousness that we are, decide to look inward to realize this balance. We must choose it.

We are called to turn back from the details and look to the whole. So our collective awakening asks us to turn inward, to recognize clearly the formless, the unmanifest pole of reality in which all manifest conditions take form. We are called to see that matter is a feature of space, that material is a manifestation of spirit, that there is no existence without emptiness and no activity without rest. We are called to sense the infinite and endless potentiality within us, as an expression of which all activity temporarily emerges. We are called to realize the undivided awareness that we are, beyond the ephemeral conditions and circumstances of existence.

In much religious and spiritual architecture and art, space and silence are highlighted, brought to our attention through vast, open interiors and muted or fading sounds, like bells or singing bowls that dissolve into silence. Complementarily, space is often contoured by structures of intricately patterned shapes and silence often intimated through rituals of intricately patterned sounds. This interplay awakens our experience of the formless, of our undivided nature within a relative expression of patterned form. It is a symbolic representation of inner balance that brings our attention to the living simplicity of spacious awareness hiding in plain sight.

Looking toward such balance, we might practice contemplating space or silence, the sensible dimensions of the formless. We may look to vistas of space in nature, to the sky or to open plains. We may seek out quiet, or listen to it underlying sounds, taking a cue from classical composer Claude Debussy, who said that "music is the space between the notes." We might look always to the unmanifest simplicity amid all the complex structure of the world.

The Experience of Presence

As you disengage from the mind and enter a state of simple awareness, the world around you awakens in you, too. So a meditative walk—a walk in a state of basic connectedness—is always a revelatory experience. Even in a grey city each form comes alive, and you can sense its immediacy, its articulation, its being. So a park's lamppost glimmers as sunlight streaks its hard contour; each of the panes of its hexagonal glass case reflects the muted speckle of swaying tree leaves. So the sounds of fireworks burst and rumble, turning in on themselves like rolling clouds and trailing into each new, bright eruption. So the fine winter branches of a young tree

undividing

spread like inverted tendrils, hard and tight, traced by the immanent stillness of light and shadow. So water's surface is smooth and clean, prickled with tiny peaks and swathes of reflected sky that find themselves in one iridescent glow. Words are insufficient as the depth of presence shines in each thing, in each expression of underlying oneness.

Connectedness or oneness may sound vague, but in oneness everything emerges in its greatest detail and proclaims its deepest particularity. Just as we come to love others through seeing past surfaces, into their hearts, and by that profound abstraction of unconditional love, adore all their details and idiosyncrasies more fiercely—their smile, their laugh, even the furrowed brow of their tired frustration—so all things approach you more fondly, more personally, as you renounce them and look into the heart of meditation. Paradoxically, in the quiet of inner awareness, disinvested from the forms of the world, you find closer contact with those very forms.

So the individual is not lost, but affirmed, in oneness. All the unique characteristics of every entity manifest themselves most clearly in the light of their own heart. Seeing them from the inside out, you see depth of particular expression. The qualitative aspects of each form stand out in crystalline detail, piercingly clear and solid, with their roots in an undivided and formless eternity. So a dry, winter leaf is brittle and beige, and its hardened veins contain a fragile face, pricked by spots of dirt. A black ant trickles over it with determined purpose, and suddenly the erratic shoots of grass around it emerge as an expansive wilderness. Some steps away a swirl of circling insects sways as a cloud of tiny points, ablaze with the weakened glare of a low sun's light.

So the formless invigorates and elucidates form, and forms intimate and partake in the formless. But there is no sense in making this a doctrine or philosophy. Move into the direct experience within you and come to see each thing bloom of its own nature. Through undivided awareness, come so intimately into contact with the forms around you that there is no space in your mind for doctrines or philosophies. So, finding yourself in the heart of all things, fall in love with the world through resolving yourself into the timeless clarity beyond it. As expressed by Zen master Dogen, "see that all the universe is one bright pearl;" in the words of Christ, "inherit the earth."

Practice for yourself: feel out the world, disinvested from the filter of mind. Its presence may be very subtle at first, but trust it. Little by little, you will come to sense the beauty and infinite immediacy of things.

Practicing Awareness

Look, throughout your day, for the subtlest glimmers of inadvertent vibrancy. Pay attention to your inner state, and relax into that very awareness, coming to know it as yourself. Whether you feel peace, pain, agitation, confusion, anxiety, excitement, sadness, anger, or joy, let your experience take a secondary focus, and look to the experiencing awareness itself. Step back from constant hurry and motion, and, for moments, disinvest from all the crazy dictates of a world lost in form.

Take a moment as you wash dishes to feel the water run over your hands, noticing its temperature and texture. Watch it part and join around objects, running in streams toward a common end. Watch the small bubbles it forms slip easily in and out of existence, now wholly present, now no more.

Getting dressed, listen intently to the rustling of clothing as its threads brush over your skin. Feel the buoyant embrace of a clean shirt as you disappear into it, pushing your head through to a quiet room. Notice each bright burst of regular activity, and the punctuating containment of silence.

Stop in your workday to look at an indoor plant, or some light filtering through a window. Let go of thoughts, of the day, of time, and sense the eternal simplicity of life for a single moment. Sense the plant, its being and vitality. Feel the still and total quality of light as it meets your intuition, easy and natural. Let this moment be an opening to the totality of undivided awareness.

Look around you, even in traffic. See the sky and the clouds, their lumbering immanence, soft and present. In grey skies, in rain, in evening light, notice attentively the qualities of each feature of infinity, and let them take you into their heart, into your heart. Let the night take you into its folds, enveloping you in its darkness of rich and muted quiet, tender and luxurious, gentle and sweeping. Be still, and let the formless reach you through all the patient vibrancy of its expressions.

Look to inner quiet like a lifelong friend, knowing it's there, trusting its presence. Find it in private moments like a secret lover, returning to its kiss, to hidden intimacy, letting such brief encounters punctuate all the activity of your days and form the sporadic rhythm of your experience. Find it anxiously, playfully. Let yourself be moved, and enjoy deepening self-discovery.

the union of form and formlessness

There is structure, and there is beauty. There is form and formlessness. Disengage from the mind and let things be as they are. Return to a natural practice of self-awareness, self-knowing, not acting on the world, but letting it act simply through you. If only for moments, abandon effort, let go, and be. Forget about the circumstances of life, and recognize that at root, you are always amid the same context of infinite awareness. Sense that body, mind, and all circumstances are only features, temporary conditions, and that you are much deeper. So disinvest, and find yourself moved by the eternal indivision of all things. In still awareness come to know with clarity the immeasurable vastness of yourself, beyond the relative experience of form.

ACKNOWLEDGEMENTS

The first draft of this book emerged almost instantaneously, and when I began writing I didn't stop until the end. But the process of making a rough draft into a finished book was much more laborious and could not have happened without the selfless involvement of others. Gratitude is an overabundant feeling, and I am moved to write so many thanks.

I am deeply grateful to my friend and editor, Caitlin Timmons, for carefully considering each word of this book and clarifying its meaning. She has participated intimately in the creation of every finished page, and I know that for both of us this has been a labor of love and an exciting way to give beautiful and concrete form to inner feeling. There is a sort of fullness like gratitude in the movement of creation itself that she has known as well as I, and that is worth more than any thanks I can offer.

Still, I so appreciate her dedication and attention to something that as of yet has no certain audience, no clear worldly value, no reasonable outward path. Together we have made a sand mandala, a sincere and cared-for work with indefinite purpose, and I am grateful for her company.

My husband Silvio Martinez has, as always, offered a sturdy and silent support that makes all things possible. The patience and ease with which he approaches each day have set the gentle pace of our lives and nurtured a steady creative rhythm. I am so fortunate to be as moved by the small spontaneities of our daily routine as I am by any creative rush, and to have a partner who will feel out the authenticity of any paragraph as we take out the trash. With simple and constant presence, he gives balance, discernment, and the encouragement to continue. His quiet energy, his way, permeates my entire life and these pages immeasurably.

My lifelong friend Andrew McCall has also moved this book along with his invariable faith in it and an ever-helping hand. He has weighed so many passages and questions that have come up during this process. Bringing pages of writing into a finished book involves unexpected layers of work, many of them related to marketing or to raw appearance and appeal. Does this section read naturally to an audience unfamiliar with the vocabulary of contemporary spirituality or ancient philosophy? Does this cover, this blurb, this website, speak to the general spirit behind it? Andrew has worked with me through every consideration with steady support, enthusiasm, and generosity.

Francesca Gratta, my friend and publicist, has given considered direction, especially during the mature stages of this creation. She has a passion for communicating and for reaching people that has shaped a lot of the most extroverted elements of this process. Like a sort of midwife of creative birth, she has guided this book's outward gaze, coaxing it into more accessible form. Through her I see it start to take

acknowledgements

on its own, independent life, and I am so grateful for her courage and care.

Many others have offered considerate advice to mold these pages. I thank friend and editor Barbara Timmons for weeding a rough draft and making it more. Her kind and careful comments quickly cut through many rough edges, softening and opening content and style. I am grateful to friend and art curator Emiliana Scaramella; her suggestions for this cover art made it shine. I thank friends Roger Bourassa, Steve Breed and Henning Fuellers for the conversation that got me started. I am grateful to my cousin Chad Detwiler and to my dear friend Shona Keir for their encouragement and enthusiasm; to my brother Liam and my whole extended family for their love and support; and to Buenos Aires, for giving this book a creative ground of such welcome and warmth. What a joy this has been!

www.ingramcontent.com/pod-product-compliance
Lightning Source LLC
Chambersburg PA
CBHW071349080526
44587CB00017B/3028